D0930540

MARCMÁRQUEZ

DREAMS COME TRUE: MY STORY

1 3 5 7 9 10 8 6 4 2

This edition published in 2014 by Ebury Press, an imprint of Ebury Publishing
A Random House Group company
First published in Spain by Editorial Planeta in 2014

Photography © Mirco Lazzari
Text © Emilio Pérez de Rozas
Foreword © Freddie Spencer

Translation by Jethro Soutar

The Random House Group Limited Reg. No. 954009

Addresses for companies within the Random House Group can be found at
www.randomhouse.co.uk

A CIP catalogue record for this book is available from the British Library

The Random House Group Limited supports the Forest Stewardship Council® (FSC®),
the leading international forest-certification organisation. Our books carrying the FSC label are
printed on FSC®-certified paper. FSC is the only forest-certification scheme supported by
the leading environmental organisations, including Greenpeace. Our paper procurement
policy can be found at www.randomhouse.co.uk/environment

Printed and bound in Italy by Rotolito Lombarda SpA

ISBN 9780091960391

To buy books by your favourite authors and register for offers visit www.randomhouse.co.uk

MARCMÁRQUEZ
DREAMS COME TRUE: MY STORY

Foreword by
Freddie Spencer

Words by
Emilio Pérez de Rozas

Photos by
Mirco Lazzari

EBURY
PRESS

Contents

Foreword Intersecting Lives

My take on Marc Márquez, 2013 MotoGP world champion

by Freddie Spencer

In the early 1920s, a young man, the son of a blacksmith who owned a bicycle shop in Japan, noticed an ad for Tokyo Art Shokai, a company that dealt in the 'Manufacture and Repair of Automobiles, Motorcycles and Gasoline Engines'. He wrote them a letter. In the late 1970s, a

young racer in the United States saw Mr Soichiro Honda and his racing team on ABC's *Wide World of Sports*. He saw a glimpse. In the late 1990s, a four-year-old boy in Spain asked his parents for a motorcycle. He was on his way. Three people from three parts of the world, three individual journeys, three paths that crossed.

Marc Márquez and I met for the first time last June. He was doing an appearance for Alpinestars in Bordeaux, France, on 7 June, and I was scheduled to be at a Honda dealer on 8 June – literally right across the alley. It just happened.

Casey Stoner had set the wheels in motion when he announced his retirement from racing at the end of the 2012 MotoGP season. As Marc was on his way to the Moto2 Championship that same year, I watched a few races. I could see this real drive and a great ability to control the bike on the edge and a little bit beyond, and to be able to do it lap after lap. In Marc's first race on a MotoGP bike, in Qatar, Jorge Lorenzo took the lead early and had the race under control. Márquez and Dani Pedrosa were battling for second when Valentino Rossi passed them both. Marc stayed with Valentino, a good sign that he could pick up the pace when needed. A podium in his first MotoGP race was kind of a barometer of how the season would go; he would just get stronger and stronger.

One of Marc's main assets is that he is very good under braking and direction changes. In my early racing career, that's something I constantly worked on: the decisiveness, the ability to quickly change direction while applying lean angle – putting the bike in position sooner rather than later to be able to accelerate. The riders who did that best this year were Márquez and Lorenzo, first and second.

At the new Circuit of The Americas in Austin, Márquez got the holeshot, got in a little deep in turn one, and ran wide. Dani got by him, but after he followed Dani for a few laps, Marc made the pass. He won the race and broke my record for youngest MotoGP race winner, one day after setting a new record for youngest rider to win pole position. Auspiciously, I watched that race while attending a classic event at Imola, the Italian circuit where in 1983 I won my first 500cc Championship and broke Mike Hailwood's record for youngest champion. That night, sitting with Phil Read watching the race, I had a feeling.

On 10 November, Márquez took third in the final round at Valencia to secure the MotoGP world title. Going into that last race, it got interesting, and the similarities between 2013 for Marc and 1983 for me are worth noting. Marc had a big points lead that dwindled precariously with a few races to go; I had a big points lead, which Kenny Roberts whittled down toward the end. That last race of 1983, if Kenny had won, I had to finish no worse than second; to win his World Championship Marc had to place no worse than fourth. During the race, Jorge's strategy was obvious: Valencia is a track that is not easy to pass on, similar to Imola in my day. You could see he slowed the pace (just like Kenny did) to keep the race close and increase the opportunity for another rider to get between him and Marc. But Marc played it smart and took third. I knew I had two seasons to break Hailwood's record to be the youngest world champion, and Marc also had two years. Destiny. I trust it. History does repeat itself; it all had to happen.

That is what I think about, what we all care about: the history, the respect for tradition. What lays out the path that gets you to Mr Honda's home? This is why we have records, so we can share the history and mark the milestones. I could tell right away that Marc understood his place in that. He is not afraid; he isn't going to back down. He perseveres, struggles, crashes, and always comes through in the race. That persevering is the drive, the spiritual side that wills us along.

My only regret is that Marc didn't win in Japan. I was at the Japanese Grand Prix and would have gotten to congratulate him on the spot. I only got to meet Hailwood once, at the Match Races in 1980. After I won at Brands Hatch on Good Friday, the press was already comparing me to Mike. I apologised to him for that because I hadn't done anything yet. Three years later, when I did win the championship, I thought how nice it would have been if he'd still been around. He was a kind person, and I believe he would have been genuinely happy for me. Thirty years on, when I saw Marc and said good luck, it was nice I could be there for him. We belong to a pretty unique club.

Only a few, based on sheer mathematics and odds, can achieve the greatness of Mr Honda or Marc Márquez. Somebody's best is going to be winning a world championship; another's best is less noticeable but no less important. It is the people, the connection, that matters. The impact of the

Freddie Spencer at Donington Park, 1984.

'My only regret is that Marc didn't win in Japan. I was at the Japanese Grand Prix and would have gotten to congratulate him on the spot.'

Mike Powell/Getty Images

individual pursuits of each of us is shared by the collective whole. Being youngest world champion at anything reminds us of the purity we all began life with, the importance of being childlike in our striving without fear of failure, nothing but true belief in the possibility, the willingness to hold the gas on in the face of doubt. Words can't describe the transition of light in the clouds once the sun sets over the ocean. Like the sun, we all have a path, a purpose, a responsibility. Thank you, Marc, for reminding us why we watch the sunset.

(Autograph says: With Love – For Marc! All the Best!)

FREDDIE SPENCER

Born in Shreveport, Louisiana, on 20 December 1961, Freddie Spencer is considered one of the top 10 riders in history. He won three world speed titles – one in the 250cc category (1985) and two in 500cc (1983 and 1985) – and earned worldwide acclaim by winning both categories in the same year, an outstanding double feat. In 1985, riding for Honda, 'Fast'

Freddie would climb off his two-and-a-half and get straight on board his five hundred, on several occasions winning races in both categories on the same day. In 2013, Spencer's name was on everyone's lips, as motorcycling fans, riders, writers and other inhabitants of the paddock watched Marc Márquez break a series of 'youngest-ever' senior class records, records that had

previously belonged to Spencer: becoming the youngest world champion in history (Marc won it aged 20 years and 266 days; Spencer won it aged 21 years and 258 days), as well as the youngest rider to set the fastest race lap (Qatar), to take pole position (Austin), to win a race (Austin) and to win back-to-back races (Sachsenring and Laguna Seca).

The Champion Smile

It was 23 February. The party was over, but only for that evening. The real party – the festival of speed, the record-breaking run, the first glory year of Marc Márquez, the best newcomer in the history of motorcycling – was about to begin.

Marc had just been presented as Repsol Honda's latest MotoGP rider. As the room emptied, Márquez was gathering his equipment from the stage when somebody suddenly appeared from out of the shadows at the back: Grandad Ramon. Marc spent much of his childhood in the company of his grandfather – his '*Avi*' – while his mother, Roser, and his father, Julià, slaved away at work.

Grandad Ramon is a typical grandad and he didn't want to miss his grandson's presentation as a premier class rider, much less miss out on the chance to see up close, even touch, his grandson's new motorbike. Grandad Ramon is Marc's number one fan and his principal accomplice. It is a relationship born of long walks together around Cervera (near Lleida, in Catalonia), Avi recovering from a heart scare, his grandson pedalling away beside him on a bike.

'Grandad, what are you doing here?'

'What does it look like, lad? I've come to check out the new "mule" they've given you.'

'Do you think I'll be able to ride it, Grandad?'

'You can do anything, lad, anything.'

'Look, look, *Avi*, you control everything from this panel here. Everything: braking, suspension, speed …'

'And how fast did you say this thing goes?'

'Two hundred and ten miles an hour, Grandad. It travels a bit, huh?'

'Give over, goodness me! You can tell it's bigger and more powerful than last year's, though.'

'You're not allowed on this one, Grandad.'

'Nooooooo way, this one's too big for me.'

'We'll see what happens, *Avi*, we'll see what happens.'

'Well, good luck, lad, good luck. And above all, like I always say: be fast, but be careful.'

Be careful … a piece of advice regularly given to 'El Pichilla', as Marc is known among the team. Be careful … a fairly redundant suggestion

for someone who thinks that 'when you're enjoying yourself and chasing a dream, nothing should slow you down'. Be careful ... a redundant suggestion to the youngest rider in history to win the World Championship in the premier category, shattering all the 'youngest ever' records set by Mike Hailwood, Freddie Spencer, Dani Pedrosa and Jorge Lorenzo.

Everything starts and ends with Grandad Ramon. Because for Marc Márquez, everything starts and ends with his family. His family at home and his family at the track. Because for all the factory bikes, the power, the high-tech alloying, the steel crankshafts, the computers, the electronics, the engine maps, the red-hot disc brakes, the chewing gum tyres, the £500,000 gearbox, the elbow pads worn thin from rubbing against the track, the units of horsepower on top of horsepower, Marc lives, races and wins for his families the one at home and the one at the track. He does it because

Marc shows Grandad Ramon how the computer works on his new Honda; in the other photos, he plays on his first racing bikes, including the one Father Christmas brought him when he was just four years old.

'[...] good luck. And above all, like I always say: be fast, but be careful.'

Ramon Márquez
Grandad

he knows his grandad is jumping with joy and happiness – and fear maybe, too – in his armchair back in Cervera.

'Marc has always been a good kid, and even now that he's all grown-up, there's still something of the boy in him,' says Don Ramon. 'We've never had to get cross with Marc – never! He's always been easy-going, I should know. The whole family is very proud of him.' Grandad Ramon never misses a race. It hardly matters – indeed it doesn't matter at all – that Sole, his wife, is forever telling him he's too old for such things, that it's ridiculous for him to get up in the middle of the night, sometimes not go to bed at all, just to watch his grandson on television. 'But I don't want to find out from others what my grandchildren have been up to. And anyway, if I went to bed and they were racing in Australia or wherever, the sheets would start itching me – I can't do it, I just can't. If my armchair could talk … for that armchair has seen me do all sorts. It's seen me leap in the air, even though I no longer have the strength to jump, it's seen me cry and suffer, it's heard me insult one or two people's mothers … Yes, that armchair could cause quite a drama.'

Family, at home and away from home. 'As far as my grandad's concerned, everything his grandchildren do is fantastic – everything,' says Marc. 'It doesn't matter if I tell him that some things didn't go so well: the way he

MARC MÁRQUEZ   MARC MÁRQUEZ   MARC MÁRQUEZ

MARC MÁRQUEZ   MARC MÁRQUEZ   MARC MÁRQUEZ

Three celebrations: Papá Julià, who never spends a single day away from his sons, celebrates Marc's 125cc title (Valencia, 2010) and Moto2 title (Australia, 2012) with his two boys; on the right, Mamá Roser joins the party, after her eldest has just become the youngest champion in MotoGP history (Valencia, 2013).

sees it, everything's just brilliant. Seeing him fill up with emotion when I get home, seeing him happy, that's the biggest pleasure in the world, the best reward anyone could ask for. I've already told him not to watch the races in the middle of the night, I've said enough's enough, but he just ignores me. He suffers terribly if he doesn't watch them.' Julià, who's prouder than anyone of his two boys, adds: 'When Marc or Àlex gets a good result, he even lets off firecrackers. I've told him: "Dad, you're too old for such things."' But he gets such a kick out of his grandchildren, he really does.'

This dual family grew in size at the same rate that Marc – and later Àlex – grew in stature on the track, while being good natured, affectionate, approachable, friendly and, above all, smiley, off the track. Marc's famous smile is his grandad's smile, his dad's smile, his mum's smile; as Marc says, 'It's a family trademark, part of the Márquez Alentà DNA, something that's with us from day one.' Marc believes that 'you have to be optimistic in life, you have to be positive. I prefer a smile to any other gesture. A smile reflects the good side of life. You have to go into things, even the bad moments, with a positive attitude. You have to try and spread a sense of positivity around your people. It's easier to overcome obstacles with a smile.'

The smile, the good nature, the 'can do, will do' attitude, the desire to please Grandad Ramon, Grandma Sole and Grandma Alvira, his dad Julià, his mum Roser, his brother Àlex, his manager Emilio Alzamora, his coach Santi Hernández, his Honda bosses Shuhei Nakamoto and Livio Suppo, all the people at Repsol; wanting them to be excited at the prospect of the back-to-back 125cc and Moto2 champion rewriting the record books while earning unprecedented praise for a senior class rookie – it all came together at the moment when the 2012 Moto2 season reached its conclusion at Valencia's Cheste circuit. It was a matter of getting off the Moto2 bike and on to the MotoGP Honda RC213V, which prompted a media scrum and led to an exclusive, historic, smouldering photo.

'Marc first climbed aboard the Honda on an absolute dog of a day. It was horrible: the track was all wet, it was dangerous, unpredictable. And by the third lap, he'd already broken the track record for the first section,' recalls Suppo. 'The least I could do was take a photo of the monitor with my mobile phone, and get a record of the epic feat. It was a historic day for all of us, but especially for Marc. The potential many of us had seen in

'Marc has a gift. He's not only quick, he's intelligent [...] Marc deals with difficult moments very calmly, with a smile, with uncommon good sense.'

Livio Suppo
Repsol Honda Team Manager

Livio Suppo.

First day of MotoGP training, early November, 2012. Cheste, Valencia.

Next page: Emilio Alzamora looks on thoughtfully as Marc talks to his coach, Santi Hernández, at the Japanese Grand Prix at Motegi.

Marc had been fulfilled in a matter of minutes. For Marc has a gift. He's not only quick, he's intelligent with it. And he can handle pressure too, because that was a tough day – it was no walk in the park! Marc deals with difficult moments very calmly, with a smile, with uncommon good sense. That smile, which is a sign of his optimism, is his greatest strength, his biggest attribute. With character and determination like that, he can overcome anything, however difficult.'

That debut ride at Cheste was very special, though Marc doesn't attach much importance to it. 'When you move up into a new category, your first task is to put yourself in control of the situation, work out how the bike handles, understand it, ask questions of it, watch, learn. No one put any pressure on me. I had a two-year contract and Nakamoto, the boss, told me to take it easy – that's right! – he said to take it easy, but he also immediately added that he thought I'd make the podium in the first race in Qatar,' says Marc, before bursting into fits of laughter.

'There are lots of riders, really a great many, who can ride a bike fast. You could pick any one of them in terms of speed, pure speed, but going fast is only one of the attributes you need in a champion,' says Alzamora, when asked about the methods and qualities that make his star pupil so outstanding. 'What makes Marc truly great is his collection of attributes, which includes his personality and the way he interacts with his family, team and colleagues, as well as his great professionalism and thoroughness, and his huge talent, of course, an innate talent for what line to take, for knowing what's happening to him on the bike and for transmitting that understanding to the engineers, then knowing how to make the most of whatever improvements have been made.'

Alzamora believes that Marc's quickness to learn and capacity to fight, along with his humility, sense of sacrifice, professionalism and wisdom – whereby he understands he's the leader of a project, the one who does the donkey work and makes the decisions on the bike – 'made everyone think, "Once he's got the bike under control and got used to the way the senior category works, he's going to achieve great things." The title? Well, I don't think anyone thought of the title at that point. Over the years, we've learned anything's possible with Marc, but I never thought of the title, not until we'd passed the mid-point of the season and I saw that he was controlling the bike, the bike wasn't controlling him, and then, yes, I did sense he could do it.'

Looking back, Márquez identifies a couple of moments as being crucial stages in his apprenticeship, as he graduated from Moto2 to MotoGP. While these moments may not have been decisive in themselves, for him they were signs of the progress he was making in adapting to the new category. 'The first thing was figuring out where I was and how things worked in MotoGP. I'd come from categories where, when I came into the pit, I talked to my coach and told him my impressions. And that was basically it. Now, when I come into the workshop, a horde of engineers, repairmen and mechanics descend upon me, Santi [Hernández] among them, of course. And I have to talk to them all, about everything, and separately: engine, telemetry, suspension, stability, tyres … And all this – this new system of working – I learned in a

'When he lifted up the visor on his helmet, I saw this mischievous smile, these shining eyes and the look of satisfaction on his face, for that fantastic lap he'd just put in. [...] It was obvious he'd had a great time out there, that he'd really enjoyed it.'

Santi Hernández
Head Coach

private test with Álvaro Bautista, a test set up specifically for me to learn how to work in MotoGP. It was a vital lesson.'

The next key moment made a strong impression on the Honda bosses, who are always very encouraging, but prudent too; afterwards, they realised exactly what sort of rider they had on their hands. The moment came in the second series of private pre-season tests in Sepang, Malaysia, when Marc fell off for a third time: three accidents in three days. 'At the end of every session we have a meeting in the pit where we sum up everything we've done,' Marc explains. 'This time, Takeo Yokoyama, a Japanese engineer, leader of the RC213V project, told me to calm down, told me I didn't need to force things so much, that I needn't take so many risks – that he didn't like me falling off and I should be more careful. To be honest, I guess he was telling me to slow down. Yes, that was it really, he was telling me to slow down.' Those present describe the look on Marc's face as a mixture of perplexity, understanding and politeness. But what the rookie said was blunt.

'I'm sorry, Takeo,' Marc recalls telling the project leader. 'I understand you, I follow your logic perfectly, but you need to understand that this is my style, and it will go on being my style. I don't fall off because I want to; I fall

'I never thought of the title, not until we'd passed the mid-point of the season and I saw that he was controlling the bike, the bike wasn't controlling him, and then, yes, I did sense he could do it.'

Emilio Alzamora
Manager and former
125cc world champion

Santi Hernández.

Carlos Liñán.

off because it's the only way I know of finding the limits. And if I want to win, if we want to win, there's no other way of us progressing, of us improving and getting faster. I'm not trying to fall off, Takeo; if I think I'm going to fall, I slow down. But just so you know, I'll keep on pushing it, because that's what training is for: getting to know the limits, my limits and the bike's limits.' Those present say the look of perplexity and understanding, or whatever it was, moved to Yokoyama's face. They exchanged knowing smiles, before Yokoyama added: 'I understand you, but you should know we're worried about you hurting yourself. We're not worried about the bike – you can break the bike and go through hundreds of spare parts, don't worry about that – but we're worried about your safety.'

Santi Hernández, Marc's coach, and Carlos Liñán, at the time Marc's most trusted mechanic, now his head mechanic, both witnessed that frank but friendly exchange, a clarifying conversation between the kindly Takeo and the somewhat bruised Marc, in the pit at Sepang. Hernández would perhaps have recalled the look of happiness on Marc's face when he brought the Honda in on that first wintry day in Cheste. 'When he lifted up the visor on his helmet, I saw this mischievous smile, these shining eyes and the look of satisfaction on his face, for that fantastic lap he'd just put in. "Santi," he said, "this here, this here's a racing bike." It was obvious he'd had a great time out there, that he'd really enjoyed it.' And Hernández immediately thought: 'We're going to have fun this year.'

Liñán offers the following assessment: 'Marc's strength is in his head, in his mind, in his well-equipped brain. Like Emilio [Alzamora] said, there are plenty of riders who can go fast, loads of them, but you can count on the fingers of one hand the ones who know why they're going fast, and there are fewer still who are able to explain to their engineers what happens to them when they're going fast on the bike. Marc does all this, and then when he goes out on the bike you've prepared for him, he gives it everything. And if it's missing anything, he finds a way round it, because he's also brilliant at managing any shortcomings the bike might have, and at controlling it, of course, as well as controlling the shape of the race in what I like to call "Matrix-style 3D". It's worth repeating: that brain of his makes decisions in milliseconds. And they're almost always the right ones.'

Throughout this transitional period, the initial contact stages, Márquez's rivals watched him and monitored his progress, day by day. Logically, some paid more attention than others. Valentino Rossi, for example, had been an admirer for a while, ever since meeting Marc back in 2008: the young lad from Cervera had shown up at the Italian champion's tent to present Rossi with a Scalextric model of a Subaru Impreza, the car 'Il Dottore' – The Doctor – had rally-driven that year (Márquez was sponsored by the toy manufacturer at the time). 'Rossi has always been very kind to me, he's always kept an eye out for me and for what I've been doing,' says Márquez. 'In my first season riding in the World Championship, when I'd finish fifteenth or twentieth in 125cc, he'd always greet me by name if we crossed paths in the paddock. I was honestly blown away.'

After that training session in Sepang, when Takeo and Marc had their friendly exchange of opinions, Rossi went out for dinner in Kuala Lumpur with Enrico Borghi, an Italian journalist friend, author of a 2005 authorised biography of The Doctor. That morning, Márquez had been second fastest, only 44 milliseconds off Dani Pedrosa. 'We've got until Brno to come up with a way of slowing Márquez down,' Rossi told Borghi that night over dessert. 'If we haven't come up with a formula for stopping him by then, we won't see him for dust.' The words of a true champion, a legend, thought Borghi.

The Catalonia Grand Prix, 2008. Marc, who had never met Valentino Rossi before and was desperate to do so, asked photographer Jaime Olivares and the author to accompany him as he went to present the Italian champion with a model toy car. And thus the historic encounter took place. 'So you're the brave Marc, great. I hope they're treating you well in the World Championship. You just let me know if they don't, I've got a bit of influence around here!' Rossi said to the young Márquez through fits of laughter.

The Party Starts'

And so the World Championship caravan made its way to Qatar, where the whole carnival would begin. A few days earlier, Márquez had been outstanding in two days of private testing in Austin, Texas, a circuit where MotoGP bikes had never run before. But Marc landed in Doha only to be given the same advice he'd heard weeks ago from Nakamoto, Suppo, Alzamora and Hernández: it's your first year, Dani Pedrosa is the one who should be up front battling for the title, don't try going too fast, take your time, make steady progress, don't obsess about trying to come first … But Marc had adapted rather well to MotoGP.

'This bike,' he would tell anyone in the team's inner circle who'd listen, 'is nothing like a Moto2 bike. This is a real racing bike. It's got more power, it's harder to understand and fine tune to suit each race, but all you have to do is take hold of it and fast times come all by themselves. This bike doesn't vibrate, it doesn't jump, it doesn't complicate your life, you don't even notice it weighs 20 kilos more than a Moto2 bike. Sure, riding it to the limit is harder, but even when riding it for fun, just to get to know it, you set good times.'

Besides, Márquez had settled into his new team brilliantly, revolutionising the life of the whole squad with his sense of engagement and his smile – and, above all else, by always being in the pit. 'Marc spends the whole day with us,' says Liñán. 'He is, without doubt, the driver who spends the least time in his motorhome. Why? Because Marc doesn't just like riding, he likes racing in general and he likes sharing the experience with his people, with his other family.' Hernández picks up on that last bit: 'When Marc says the team is his "other family", he means it.'

Qatar was a nervy weekend – how could it not be! Marc was making his debut among the 'heavyweights'. 'First comes the official photo with everyone, and there I am in the middle, sharing the stage with riders I've admired for years,' Márquez recalls. Meanwhile Colin Edwards was busy filming everything with his video camera. ('But this doesn't mean it's my last season,' said the Texan. However, Edwards, who had turned forty and was a MotoGP fixture, stood down from the Yamaha NGM Forward Racing team in 2014.) 'To be honest, it was a very emotional moment, and then to top it all off, there's the group press conference and, due to nerves, my English wouldn't come out properly.'

'Marc spends the whole day with us. [...] Marc doesn't just like riding, he likes racing in general and he likes sharing the experience with his people, with his other family.'

Carlos Liñán
Head Mechanic

The Qatar Grand Prix, the first race of the 2013 season. Jorge Lorenzo won and Marc finished third, making the podium on his MotoGP debut, just as Honda's boss Shuhei Nakamoto had predicted.

Márquez acknowledges that he was making his debut both on and off the track, taking his lead from the others. 'Being the novice, that's the way it ought to be, right?' To give himself a boost before going to the hotel, Marc put on fresh tyres for the last few test laps and managed to clock a good time. It was a way of psyching himself up. 'But everyone knew that time was misleading – pure trickery.' Which is why he ignored the praise. Marc didn't know it, but that first Friday in Qatar, Rossi dined with Borghi again, this time in the luxury restaurant of his hotel in Doha. After the great time Márquez had registered, Rossi told Borghi: 'Forget it, Enrico, it's too late to slow Marc down. That kid will have us all beaten before we reach Brno. There's nothing we can do about it. He's brilliant. That kid's here to stay, and I'm telling you, he wants to win it this year, even if he won't admit it.'

But Sunday was still fraught with uncertainties for Marc. 'I was the only one who could put hard tyres on at the rear, but we decided to put soft ones on like everyone else.' He got off to a bad start ('setting a pattern for the whole season') and the better riders escaped. Márquez decided not to look at the scoreboard. 'I looked only at the lap counter. I was obsessed with chasing down Dani, until I caught him.' Everyone was left open-mouthed as an amazing duel ensued: two desert hawks in the Qatari night.

'I was right there with them, with Jorge, with Dani – with Valentino even! It was mind-blowing to me,' recounts Márquez. 'I was very nervous, but I was also really enjoying it. Suddenly – wham! – Rossi passes me, and I say to myself, 'Wow, that was Vale!' And I chase after him. And I pass him, and he passes me again, naturally, because Valentino is Valentino. But anyway, I'd set out to finish as the first Honda in the first grand prix.' And this he duly managed, coming in third behind Lorenzo and Rossi. Nakamoto was right: a podium finish in his first grand prix.

The 'big circus' then jumped over to the United States, to the new circuit in Austin. 'I arrived very excited, extremely excited, because I knew the private testing sessions we'd done there had gone very well. But it's one thing training and a very different thing riding in a GP,' Márquez concedes. Especially if, on your very first practice run, you end up flying through the air because the bike has violently unseated you. 'It was my first fall "MotoGP style",' says Márquez, 'by which I mean being launched over the windscreen and dumped on the tarmac. Up until then, I'd always fallen because the bike had shot off forward and – whack! – I'd come off the back; I'd never flown over the top before.' And it hurt. A lot.

Pain, yes, but conviction, confidence, determination. And four new 'youngest ever' records: pole, victory, championship leader and top of the podium, this time in MotoGP. 'The circuit was perfect for our Honda and off we went, Dani and I. I didn't think I had the strength, the capacity or experience to lead the race, so I decided to ride behind Dani, to learn, and I only put in a spurt at the end, to pass him and win. To be honest, after overtaking him, I went flat out for three or four laps to try and open up a

Marc's first MotoGP victory, at Austin, Texas. From left to right: Emilio Alzamora, Santi Hernández, Bruno Leoni, Christian Gabarrini, Carlo Liuzzi, Giulio Nava, Marc, Andrea 'Mondo' Brunetti, Klaus Nöhles (Bridgestone technician), Carlos Liñán, Roberto 'Ginetto' Clerici, Andy Dawson (Ohlins technician) and Filippo Brunetti.

gap, to give myself a cushion, but the bike kept giving me nasty shocks. I don't know why. I couldn't understand it.' When he crossed the finishing line as winner and came into the paddock, amid scenes of joy and celebration, Marc reported the problem to Hernández, who pointed down at the front wheel and showed Marc that one side of the tyre was 'totally wrecked'. They still don't know how it happened.

That win left Nakamoto lost for words. 'To be honest, I'd been impressed with the way Marc had conducted himself right from the start of the World Championship,' says the HRC (Honda Racing Corporation) circuit manager. 'After he'd won in 125cc, and while he was battling it out for the Moto2 title in 2011, I approached him and told him if he decided to take the leap into MotoGP in 2012, we'd have a factory bike ready for him. Marc thanked me but said he wanted to enter MotoGP only after winning the Moto2 title.' Although Nakamoto had predicted a podium place in Qatar, he hadn't expected Márquez to win a race so soon. 'I didn't think Marc would be challenging Jorge and Dani until well into the season. Winning in Austin was unthinkable as far as I was concerned. And not just me: the whole team. We were all asking ourselves how he'd managed it.'

Suppo sees that victory as proof that Marc is 'a genuine phenomenon' – it was so unexpected and yet so authoritative. 'That day, I remembered something Rossi had told me: that he'd never considered the possibility of winning the title in his first year in the premier category (2000), but that it had been a mistake – now that he was seeing how brilliantly Marc was performing as a rookie, he regretted not having really gone for it. Clearly those who'd asked Marc to take it easy in his first races weren't aware of who they were talking to, for this guy knows what he can handle better than anybody,' says Suppo.

Mick Doohan, considered one of the all-time greats and a rider who was dominant throughout his career, agrees that this early victory was a defining moment in Marc's development, but more importantly he sees it as a defining moment in terms of the championship, for the effect it had on his rivals. 'Winning so soon showed everyone who Marc was, what his objectives were and, above all else, it put fear into his opponents. Because it wasn't just the fact that he won, it was the way he won, the convincing nature of it, dominating every day and taking charge of the race with total authority. Plus the speed in which he achieved all this, in only his second GP, meant he grew in confidence. "If I've done it once I can do it again," he'll have thought, and rightly so.'

Then it was back to Europe for a race on home soil, at Jerez, where Márquez was mobbed by everyone; the newcomer leading the championship, the boy who'd just dazzled the world. But problems emerged. Although it was a track he knew well, for some reason he struggled to get going. Only on the Saturday did he start to make progress. In the race itself, he got off to a good start – finally! – but Pedrosa escaped. Márquez got on to the back of Lorenzo and then came the duel that everyone had been waiting for.

'Winning so soon showed everyone who Marc was, what his objectives were and, above all else, it put fear into his opponents. [...] it meant he grew in confidence.'

Mick Doohan
Five-time world champion with Honda

The Indianapolis Grand Prix, a third consecutive victory for Marc, after winning at Sachsenring, in Germany, and Laguna Seca, California.

'I stayed behind Jorge and observed him. He brakes in a very particular manner, very different to the way I do, or the way Danny does, or Vale. Jorge brakes early but not fully, he doesn't hammer on the brakes, he squeezes them, braking gradually, prolonging it, and not always at the same place. All of this confused me a great deal,' says Márquez.

So much so that the race came down to the last lap and the final corner, curiously the very corner that had been named after Lorenzo in a ceremony the previous day. That hairpin bend was the last chance of the day. Pedrosa was going to win, but Márquez wanted the 'silver medal'. He had already tried to overtake Lorenzo on the sharp turn leading into the back straight. 'My front wheel sensor was showing I was risking coming off, but I had to try it. As we got to the last corner, I saw Jorge had opened up a little. I knew that I braked later than him and more sharply. So I thought: "I'll give it a go, come on." And I started thinking that maybe I'd gone too far over, as can happen in such manoeuvres, and that he'd gain ground on the inside and come straight back past me. But then I saw Jorge was closing me off, so there was no option but to hang on in there, to tense the body and legs and think: "It's in God's hands now." And yes, we did touch, but we didn't fall. And I ended up in front of him.'

Márquez thought for an instant about Valentino Rossi, Sete Gibernau, Dani Pedrosa, Àlex Crivillé, Mick Doohan … all the riders who had won or lost on that same hairpin, who'd attacked or been attacked, but experienced it one way or the other, just as he and Lorenzo were experiencing it now. 'I'd resigned myself to third place, but Jorge opened the door and it was too tempting. Last lap, last corner, Jerez, my MotoGP debut season, my people – and he opened the door … I couldn't help myself!' Lorenzo refused to shake Marc's hand in the paddock afterwards, wagging the finger of his right hand as if to say 'No, no, no, not like that', Marc recalls. 'And not only in front of the TV cameras either. Afterwards, when we were on our own, I went to look for him, but he still wouldn't accept my apology.'

There was quite a storm. There were calls to sanction Márquez for what many people saw as over-aggressive riding. 'If we'd fallen, they'd have maybe tried to impose a sanction. I was acting right on the limits of what's permitted, but it was the last lap and the last corner,' Marc points out. And not all the comment was critical. 'I can't remember a rookie rider as good

Photographs courtesy of Yamaha Press

The overtake. The sequence on the left captures the historic moment, on the last corner at Jerez, when Marc seized the chance to take second place from Jorge Lorenzo, who refused to shake Marc's hand in the paddock afterwards (right).

Courtesy of MotoGP.com/Niki Kovács

'I can't remember a rookie rider as good as Marc – he's able to do things on the track the rest of us aren't capable of doing. [...] Marc's come to beat us all.'

Cal Crutchlow
British rider

as Marc – he's able to do things on the track the rest of us aren't capable of doing,' said British rider Cal Crutchlow, when asked about Marc's act of daring. 'It's very difficult to compete with Marc. Even Dani, on the same bike, has trouble competing with him. I can understand how Lorenzo feels, but that's bike racing for you. I see it through Marc's eyes. Others don't see it that way and – I'll say it again – I understand the way they feel, because Marc's come to beat us all.'

What not many people know is that the following day, Monday, Márquez boarded the plane to Barcelona and saw he'd been assigned seat 7B, in the middle of the row; as he walked down the aisle, who did he see sitting in 7A? Jorge Lorenzo. 'Santi, Santi,' Marc said to Hernández, 'you've got to swap seats with me! Come on, please, man, you sit in 7B and I'll take your ticket, I'll sit by the aisle, 7C.' And this they did.

However, unfortunately there were three motorbike nuts sitting right behind them, talking non-stop, yelling even, about Márquez overtaking Lorenzo. 'What balls that lad's got,' said one. 'They say Lorenzo wouldn't even shake his hand afterwards or anything,' said another. In the end, before the whole thing got out of hand ('I thought it was going to get ugly, I really did'), Marc got up from his seat, as if to get something from his rucksack in the overhead locker. Straightaway three of them were exclaiming: 'Blimey,

Dusk at Motorland. At the Aragón circuit, Marc won his sixth race of the season, ahead of the Yamaha champions Jorge Lorenzo and Valentino Rossi.

look, it's Marc! And wow, look, it's Jorge too!' A deluge of photos followed, Marc and Jorge posing separately, of course. Once off the aeroplane, at El Prat airport, Márquez caught up with Lorenzo and told him he understood why he was angry, but said let's shake on it. Lorenzo offered Marc his hand, muttering, 'I'll shake on it, but just so you know, I'll get my own back.'

By the time they reached Le Mans, the handshake had become public knowledge. And that was that – end of story. The French Grand Prix was the future champion's first taste of racing in the wet, but after a dreadful start ('My wheel just skidded and skidded for several seconds'), Márquez made up ground and earned himself another podium finish, in a race won by Pedrosa. Marc recognises that the first time he rode the Honda in the wet, in Jerez, he suffered big time ('I bottled it, I admit that') so making the podium at Le Mans tasted like success. 'That race was a sort of badge of honour, because to come third in your first MotoGP race in the wet is a tremendous achievement,' says Liñán. 'I think Marc left France, with that trademark smile of his, thinking: "From now on, it can rain all it likes."'

He came back down to earth with a bump at Mugello, Italy – a very dangerous bump with a miraculously happy ending. It had rained again

The start of the French Grand Prix, at Le Mans, in the rain. The photo shows Marc (Honda, 93), Nicky Hayden (Ducati, 69), Valentino Rossi (Yamaha, 46) and Dani Pedrosa (Honda, 26).

> 'This boy is learning too fast, he learns a lot riding behind me.'
>
> *Dani Pedrosa*
> *Repsol Honda rider*

and Márquez had already fallen in the first practice session on Friday. In the second session, with the track dry but very slippery in outlying areas, Marc knew that the warnings people had been giving him ('Be careful not to brake too late coming off the back straight') were right: it was extremely dangerous. 'I touched on the front brake when the wheel was still in the air and when it made contact with the tarmac it got stuck, the steering locked and I was taken suddenly off line, off the tarmac, at 175mph, and on to the slippery grass. I touched the rear brake, it kicked a bit from the back and, with the bike tipping to one side and the wall coming at me fast, I touched on the front brake and threw myself off. The bike flew into the wall and I flew towards the track.' Pure survival instinct.

Márquez remembers he got to the track hospital with his chin guard damaged and his helmet full of earth, grass and pebbles. 'I was dragged along the ground for several yards and the helmet's chin guard acted like a spade, scraping earth and stones in. I knew I hadn't broken anything and I wanted to leave the medical centre right away, but they held me round the neck and ordered me to keep still! They did a few X-rays, saw that nothing

Marc entering the medical centre at Mugello, Italy, after falling hard in practice, injuring his chin.

After his spectacular 175mph fall in practice, Marc was riding comfortably in second place when, just a few laps from the end, he suffered another fall – and a first zero on his scorecard. The photo captures his reaction.

was broken and let me leave. To be honest, that day my respect for the bike increased massively. Not fear, but respect.' In the race itself, Marc lost four-tenths of a second every time he passed the problem spot. Towards the end, by which time he'd pulled away from Pedrosa ('This boy is learning too fast, he learns a lot riding behind me,' Dani would say) but couldn't catch Lorenzo, Marc fell, losing 20 precious points. 'I was stupid, stupid, stupid. I relaxed, although I suppose the ups and downs of the whole weekend, the tiredness and the pain injections played a big part in my falling too.'

Although what happened in Mugello was a tremendous shock, Suppo was hugely impressed. 'Despite his youth, Marc showed astonishing maturity at certain moments of what was a spectacular debut season in MotoGP. He has outstanding character, and that's what makes him unique and means he can get over accidents like the one at Mugello, sliding along the ground at 175mph with the wall so close. The manner in which he dealt with that accident, the way he recovered and rode a great race, was not only a display of great professionalism, but proof that he has exceptional mental fortitude. That's what enables him to overcome these very delicate moments, which not everyone would be able to deal with so resolutely. You have to have a lot of courage and mental strength to go out and race the day after an accident like that.'

Márquez recognises that the fall in practice at Mugello, followed by the mistake that led to him losing out in the race, served as a reminder that the season was going to be tough. 'And then the comments started: that Márquez falls a lot, that Márquez is going to hurt himself, that Márquez needs to calm down … As soon as I stepped out at Montmeló, all I could think of was getting this huge weight off my shoulders.' Top priority for the Catalonia Grand Prix was to finish the race, come what may, with no incidents. 'It was a grand prix to learn from. I decided to copy Dani, although it's impossible to use the same parameters as his telemetry, totally impossible. But in that race I decided I'd brake wherever he broke and put my foot down whenever he did. And if I fell, then I fell.' But he didn't fall, and he finished third behind Lorenzo and Pedrosa. 'I learned a great deal that day. What's more, I was tempted to try and pass Dani on the last corner, but I resisted.' Well, not entirely. There was a tussle. So much so that Marc joked with Dani afterwards, saying, 'I know you don't know what happened

The relationship between the season's two giants, Marc and Jorge, ended up being cordial, despite the tension. In the image above, Lorenzo, third in Malaysia, congratulates Marc, who finished second; on the right, the press conference ahead of the Catalonia Grand Prix.

yet, but before you watch the video, let me apologise, though I didn't push it so far as to have us touch.'

Next came the Dutch Grand Prix at Assen, the legendary circuit known as the 'Cathedral'. It was here Lorenzo became the hero of the summer. 'When I came out for the first training session, I could see that something was wrong with Jorge, but I didn't give it much thought, I went past and carried along on my way. When I got back to the pit, Santi told me Jorge had come off and that it didn't look good, that he might have broken a collarbone.' And so he had. He was taken to Barcelona, had an operation and came back the very next day (in the Netherlands, you race on Saturdays). He passed a fitness test at the track clinic and came out to race.

'The courage Jorge showed that weekend was extraordinary,' says Marc. 'It was very brave of him to come out and race in those circumstances.' Lorenzo reckoned he had no choice. 'Marc was very strong and if I wanted to keep fighting for the title, I had to try and drop as few points as possible.' In the first few laps Lorenzo even fought it out with the lead riders, in spite of having just had surgery. He finished fifth, itself a tremendous feat. 'In the Netherlands it was impossible to win on a Honda, totally impossible!' concludes Márquez. 'Vale won – it had been a long time since he'd won a race – and I had to make do with second place. If Jorge had been fit, he'd have put 10 seconds on all of us!'

Lorenzo's heroics were obviously rather controversial. Many people thought the Majorcan shouldn't have been allowed to race in his condition. 'I wouldn't have ridden,' Márquez now says. 'But I also understand it's a matter of how you feel. Only you know how you are and whether you're up to it. I've never – touch wood – broken a collarbone, so I don't know what it's like. It was the sixth time Jorge had broken one, so perhaps he's more used to the recovery process. All the same, his courage deserves our admiration.' However, Márquez is adamant this has nothing to do with riders being crazy: 'You can't be crazy and travel at 200mph; quite the opposite in fact: you have to be the sanest person on earth. We see things very clearly and we know when we can and when we can't try things,' says Marc, who fell off again that weekend, hurt himself and raced with micro-fractures in the little finger of his right hand and the big toe of his left foot.

At the mountainous circuit of Sachsenring, in what used to be the German Democratic Republic, Márquez saw how, as in Mugello, fate can intervene to change the course of a race, and he could once again dream of making history – yet more history. Pedrosa hit the deck and broke a collarbone, and Lorenzo came off again too: neither of them could race. 'I was the rider who fell off the most during the whole season, but I was the only one who didn't kiss the tarmac in Sachsenring. All eyes were on me. Without Jorge or Dani, I just had to win it,' explains Marc.

And he duly did win it, though he didn't enjoy it. 'I need a battle to have a good time. I need to race, to fight, to take on the best. And that day the best were at home, injured.' Mick Doohan, a great champion and a huge admirer of Marc – one of Doohan's successors at Honda – saw it differently: 'It was the luck and strength of a champion, because Marc, as well as all his other virtues, knew how to capitalise on his rivals' moments of weakness, and that's something that makes a champion.' The person who best summed up the day was, as ever, Valentino Rossi: 'It was Marc's day, and he crushed us. Now we head for Laguna Seca, a circuit made for bastards like him.'

Laguna Seca, California, was another of the legendary venues in the 2013 World Championship. Márquez was particularly excited about the fixture, so much so that he'd trained for the race for several days, at home in Cervera with his brother Àlex, with whom he shares everything. Training consisted of endless games on PlayStation, and several hours on the computer. 'Santi had sent me the telemetry, the data, the gear ratio, everything I needed to study the circuit, the "Corkscrew", the line … everything. I prepared meticulously, though of course it's one thing to play it, another to race it.'

It was at Laguna Seca where another of the key moments (some would say *the* moment) of the season occurred: Márquez passing Rossi on the inside of the Corkscrew, a sloping bend, a twister, a dizzying spiral of a turn. 'I flatly deny that it was premeditated, that it was at all pre-planned or studied for. Of course, I'd seen the moves from previous years, some of them performed by great champions, especially Rossi on Casey Stoner in 2008. But when I went over it several times on the Thursday afternoon, on the scooter, with Santi sitting behind me, it was only to see, given that it was a blind bend, whether the hard shoulder would grip or whether it would

'Marc's like a new and improved version of Valentino Rossi. The new model Rossi.'

Valentino Rossi
Nine-time World Champion

The Dutch Grand Prix. Marc, who finished second, congratulates his hero Valentino Rossi, whose great victory at Assen put him back on top of the podium.

wreck the bike, should there be no option but to cut across it – no more than that.' No more, no less.

The fact is it happened. With Stefan Bradl having escaped after a great start, Márquez hunted down The Doctor and snared him, just as they came over the brow of the hill before the descent – the near-suicidal drop – that leads into the Corkscrew. 'Evidently the overtaking provoked Valentino.' You don't say. 'Oh yes, because I was tearing along, going very fast, and I reached the brow of the hill and I was ahead of him by half a bike as we made the turn, and by the time we'd squeezed on the brakes, I'd gained half a bike on him. But, good friend that he is, Rossi resists, loosens up on the brakes, closes in, closes in on me – totally legally! – we touch, fairing against fairing, and if there'd have been a wall, I'd have smashed into it, and if there'd have been a cliff, I'd have gone off the end of it.'

So what did Márquez do? What did Marc Márquez Alentà do? It was tremendous. 'I held firm, tensed my legs, clasped the bike between my knees, gripped the handlebars, held my breath, closed my eyes and gave it the lot! And yes, I passed him, I did a bit of motocross, just a little bit, and pulled away. We touched slightly, I managed to get through the rough and I screamed *yeeeees*! On the next curve I very nearly came off – very nearly! – because of the euphoria, the adrenaline. But then, once I'd straightened the bike up, I thought: "Now you have to go and win it – go get Bradl!"' And he got him. And he passed him. And he won it. And the world saluted the rookie to beat all rookies. And Stoner felt a sense of revenge. And Rossi smiled. And amid laughter and congratulatory hugs with his friend and tormentor, Rossi affectionately called Márquez the *piccolo bastardo*. 'How do you say it? The little bastard, no?' Yep, that's Marc.

'At Laguna Seca, Márquez went really fast, really very fast,' Rossi recalls. 'If he hadn't overtaken me on the Corkscrew, he'd have done it three turns later, so it was a rather theatrical overtaking, great choreography. But it was brilliant overtaking and it really surprised me, because I was expecting him to come up on my left and – wham! – he appeared on the inside.' Rossi rounded off his praise by saying, 'Marc's like a new and improved version of Valentino Rossi. The new model Rossi.'

That move brought worldwide admiration. 'Valentino was very smart not to get angry about that marvellous move by Márquez,' points out Giacomo

Doing the impossible. Everyone thought it was premeditated and pre-planned, but Marc denies it. The image shows the almost impossible overtake Marc performed on Valentino Rossi, on the downhill double turn known as the Corkscrew at Laguna Seca, replicating a move The Doctor himself had made on Australian rider Casey Stoner in 2008. 'Ever since that day,' Rossi recalls, 'Casey has hated me.'

'I held firm, tensed my legs, clasped the bike between my knees, gripped the handlebars, held my breath, closed my eyes and gave it the lot! And yes, I passed him, I did a bit of motocross, just a little bit, and pulled away.'

Marc Márquez

Agostini, a compatriot of The Doctor and one of the greats, with five world titles to his name. 'It would have been impossible for Vale to protest, for he'd done it himself on Stoner before, so he should know better than anybody that someone with the same talent had played him and beaten him, and at the very same spot. You have to take your hat off to Marc.' (In fact Rossi did protest, tongue in cheek, saying it was *his* move and raising the question of copyright!) Agostini goes on to add: 'With such a spectacular and cheeky overtake, Marc showed he'd lost any sense of awe for the greats. Márquez is a terrible *ragazzino*, very proud and aggressive. He's exactly the sort of champion our sport needs if it wants to stay alive.'

'Marc overtaking Vale on the Corkscrew reminds me of the goal Maradona scored with his hand,' says Suppo, a look of satisfaction on his face, like a teacher watching his brightest pupil solve a difficult maths problem. 'Depending on how you look at it, it's either an absolute masterstroke, something brilliant and marvellous, or something that really riles you. Rossi, thankfully, saw it as a masterstroke, given that he'd done the same thing to Stoner.' As one of Márquez's bosses put it: 'At Laguna Seca, the crafty, smart, cunning Marc re-emerged. That boy has a gift, a great gift: he has talent, and he's intelligent. There are those who are talented and there are those who are intelligent, and then there are those who are talented and intelligent, like Marc.'

The next date on the calendar was the original Speedway fixture: Indianapolis. It was the third US Grand Prix of the season and, as it turned out, the third victory on US soil for Márquez, who added Indy to Austin and Laguna Seca, and this time with Lorenzo and Pedrosa back to full fitness. 'That was key. We were all fit again and it was a good time to lay down another marker,' says Márquez, who in the process turned another dream into reality: being the best every day of the weekend.

That made it another unforgettable one. Fast on Friday, fast on Saturday, unstoppable on Sunday. First in training, pole in qualifying, first in the pre-race practice and invincible in the race proper, setting the fastest lap while brilliantly overtaking Pedrosa on the inside of a left turn, two laps before passing Lorenzo on the inside of a right turn, then bursting away to win the race and, in the process, amass the best points score in history by any rookie in the premier class, with the first 10 grand prix of the season completed.

'Márquez is a terrible *ragazzino*, very proud and aggressive. He's exactly the sort of champion our sport needs if it wants to stay alive.'

Giacomo Agostini
Fifteen-time world champion

'Marc overtaking Vale on the Corkscrew reminds me of the goal Maradona scored with his hand. [...] it's either an absolute masterstroke [...] or something that really riles you.'

Livio Suppo
Repsol Honda Team Manager

'Marc is like a young Valentino. [...] Riders like Márquez only come along once every 20 years: Agostini, Roberts, Spencer, Rossi ...'

Carlo Pernat
The man who discovered Rossi

Marc smiles beside Rossi at the post-race press conference at Laguna Seca. 'Marc appeared where I least expected it, but in any case, he was going so fast he'd have passed me sooner or later,' said The Doctor, acknowledging the young champion's courage and daring.

It was a victory to keep furnishing the legend. 'When I saw him overtake Vale on the Corkscrew, I sensed that what we were seeing was a sort of relay, one legend taking the baton from another, one legend on the way down and one on the way up – that basically Marc is like a young Valentino,' says the Italian Carlo Pernat, the man who discovered Rossi, and one of the most important managers in the World Championship. 'When Marc won in Indy, I no longer had any doubt: this lad is the next phenomenon. Riders like Márquez only come along once every 20 years: Giacomo Agostini (born in Brescia, Italy, 1942), Kenny 'The Martian' Roberts (Modesto, California, USA, 1951), 'Fast' Freddie Spencer (Shreveport, Louisiana, USA, 1961), Valentino Rossi (Tavullia, Pesaro e Urbino, Italy, 1979) and Marc Márquez (Cervera, Lleida, Spain, 1993).'

Brno: the Clincher

Brno is a charming circuit in the Czech Republic, a track the riders love and often use for training. It usually produces great races where all the riders do well, cheered on by tens of thousands of spectators from all over Europe. Márquez saw it as a special race, an important fixture. The Yamaha team, with Lorenzo to the fore, had done a private testing at Brno a few weeks before the race, meaning they had the edge in terms of tailoring the bike to suit the grand prix.

Sure enough, Brno proved a key chapter in this amazing story. Not just because Márquez won ahead of Dani and Jorge; not just because he notched up his fourth consecutive victory (Sachsenring, Laguna Seca, Indianapolis and Brno), something no rookie had ever achieved in the senior class before; not just because he moved clear in the World Championship standings with 213 points (to Pedrosa's 187 and Lorenzo's 167) – rather because of something Marc himself recognises: 'After the private testing we did in Motorland, it had become me leading the bike, not the bike leading me.'

Alzamora, the man Julià and Roser put in charge of Marc's sporting career when their son was only 12 years old, picks up the theme: 'Obviously, the biggest surprise for all of us was just how quickly Marc adapted to the premier category. Those of us who knew him, knew he'd achieve great things as a rookie, but the consistency he showed – he only fell once in a race, in Mugello – is what surprised me the most.'

Alzamora agrees that, for the first part of the season, it was a matter of the bike controlling the boy. 'Marc took a lot of risks in every training session because, as he explained to Yokoyama, he needed to know the bike's absolute limits. It was his way of breaking the beast in, all the while knowing he was putting himself in danger. From Brno on, Marc was in total control of the bike and everything to do with its preparation, and he started enjoying himself riding it. That's why I think he deserves enormous credit for the results he achieved in the first half of the season, because he earned those points while still learning how to ride a MotoGP bike, while doing battle with the bike, while taking control of the ship.'

Alzamora, who is there for Márquez every minute of every day, believes the attitude of the technical team, led by Santi Hernández, and the tact shown by Shuhei Nakamoto and Livio Suppo, in dealing with their rookie becoming the MotoGP man of the moment, were all fundamental factors

'To be honest, in terms of teaching Marc things, there's not much more I can teach him, he can go it alone and make his own decisions now.'

Emilio Alzamora
*Manager and former
125cc world champion*

Marc celebrates with a big smile after winning the Czech Republic Grand Prix, a race he was especially keen to win. Yamaha had been favourites after training on the Brno circuit a few days earlier.

in Marc's success. So too, of course, was 'the role played by Marc's family – Julià and Roser, but also Àlex, a great kid and a rider we'll be hearing a lot more about – in keeping Marc's feet on the ground and making sure he remained the sensible, professional, humble and hardworking person he'd always been'.

Alzamora is convinced that the best of Márquez is still to come. The manager of the triple champion is modest about his own contribution: 'I just offer him the occasional dose of peace, calm and reflection. To be honest, in terms of teaching Marc things, there's not much more I can teach him, he can go it alone and make his own decisions now.' Something that makes Marc truly exceptional, Alzamora believes, is the fact that, in the nine years they've been working together, he has never once heard Marc make excuses, 'and that makes him greater still'. Alzamora also emphasises the importance of the 'family' experiment.

It was Marc who invented the idea of the double family: one family at home, one at the track. His sense of passion and love; his great affection and devotion to Grandad Ramon: everything stems from his family. 'The two families end up being the same thing,' says Márquez, roaring with laughter. 'I like for everything in life – my life and the lives of my people and team – to be a full-on family affair. I know there are people, including a lot of riders, who don't get this, and I understand that, but I prefer it this way and, to be honest, it's always worked fantastically well for me. The collaboration is vital to me and forms a large part of the whole wonderful adventure.' Marc thinks the secret lies 'in your family knowing how to act at the circuit and your circuit-family knowing how to act away from the circuit'. That's why Marc relentlessly went about rebuilding the MotoGP pit team, a team that's now complete, with Santi Hernández, Jordi Castellà, Javier Ortiz and Hugo Bucher.

Jumping – and there is no better way of putting it – between the two camps, forming part of both families, albeit without having a bedroom in Marc's family home or a room in the pit enclosure, is one of the great Márquez family secrets: Genís Cuadros, personal trainer to both Cervera boy wonders. 'Those of us who operate around the riders, and very especially those of us who experience their day-to-day lives, have to be normal people, have to act normally and insist that they treat us normally. It's very important that they – riders who are under great strain all day, and who periodically receive excessive praise – understand that we're all just normal people, starting with themselves, of course. It would be easy for these boys to lose their bearings. But I can assure you that Marc and Àlex are both extraordinary lads, with very sensitive parents, and it's hard to imagine success, glory and fame going to their heads.'

Cuadros smiles when he explains that they don't work in 'some fancy, high-class gymnasium', but rather in a modest gym with the basic essentials – 'and if it turns out we're missing something, I go and see my mate the ironmonger and tell him to make us whatever it is'. Cuadros – who says Marc and Àlex, 'never get tired, they've never had enough, they always want more and more' – focuses mainly on flexibility. 'I'm always

'I'm always telling them I'd rather they were as flexible as cats than strong as dogs, because when a cat falls, it performs a few somersaults and almost always lands on its feet.'

Genís Cuadros
Personal trainer to Àlex and Marc

Marc's and Àlex with Genís Cuadros, their personal trainer, on one of the many bicycle rides they take in and around their hometown of Cervera.

telling them I'd rather they were as flexible as cats than strong as dogs, because when a cat falls, it performs a few somersaults and almost always lands on its feet.'

Cuadros likes repeating something he was once told by a leading personal trainer, someone who counted golfer Tiger Woods among his charges: 'You're not what you achieve, but what you know.' The point being that over the course of 18 grands prix and hundreds of laps, there will be multiple obstacles, not all of which can be overcome. 'You could argue,' says Alzamora, 'that Marc has had to deal with more difficulties in his first season in MotoGP than most riders would expect to deal with in a

For Marc's team, 2013 was a year of extreme tension and happiness, hence all the embraces and celebrations. Top left, Carlos Liñán hugs his friend Santi Hernández. Bottom left, Shuhei Nakamoto is congratulated by Italian mechanic Andrea 'Mondo' Brunetti. Top right, Liñán wipes away the tears after one of Marc's six grand prix victories. Bottom left, Marc poses smiling in the Brno paddock, with mechanics Filippo Brunetti and Bruno Leoni.

Following pages: More smiles in the paddock after Marc's victory in the German Grand Prix at Sachsenring. From left to right, Julià Márquez, Roberto 'Ginetto' Clerici, Bruno Leoni, Christian Gabarrini (at the back), Andrea 'Mondo' Brunetti, Filippo Brunetti, Carlo Liuzzi, Marc, Giulio Nava, Santi Hernández, Carlos Liñán, Emilio Alzamora (at the back) and Sylvia García from Gas Jeans.

Action from the British Grand Prix at Silverstone.

whole career, but he's managed to face up to these challenges calmly and optimistically.'

Next stop the great Silverstone circuit in England, and a race that would prove to be another baptism of fire for Márquez. He took pole, everything was shaping up nicely and then four hours before the race, in the final warm-up session, the one in which the riders try out their bikes in race configurations, Márquez crashed on the most unlikely of corners. And dislocated his left shoulder. He'd experienced this before, having done it as a child and as a teen – as an apprentice and as a champion – and so he ran to the ambulance and made straight for the track hospital.

'I knew I hadn't broken anything because, when I got up from the ground, I put my hand inside my race suit and realised my shoulder was out of place. I knew it had to be put back as soon as possible, for if you let a few minutes pass it won't recover and – most importantly – they won't let you race.' So he went into the hospital shouting: 'Where's the doctor who puts shoulders back?' But the room was in total chaos. Spanish Moto2 rider Dani Rivas had caused an unfortunate pile-up at the start line and the hospital was packed with bruised and injured riders waiting for treatment.

Márquez spotted Ángel Charte, one of the medics who follow the Spanish gladiators wherever they go. 'Ángel! Ángel! Tell the doctor to put my shoulder back! Come on, quick, please – hurry.' Charte went and found help, but the doctor who came over wanted to do it by the book: 'First we have to explore the injury, evaluate it, see exactly what you've got …'

'No evaluating, no nothing,' said Marc, 'please, just put my shoulder back, quick!' Márquez pleaded, then turned on the charm and won the doctor round. A nurse approached with some scissors, ready to cut through Marc's Repsol Honda rider's suit – 'No, no, take them away, don't cut it, I'll take it off' – and finally the doctor put the shoulder back in place. Patched up and given pain-killing injections, Marc left the clinic knowing he'd at least be able to race.

Despite the injury, it turned out to be the first great Lorenzo–Márquez head-to-head. And what a duel it was, a fantastic tussle. Immense – just like the two riders. 'I set off with the sole intention of getting in the points, but as the laps passed, I found I was feeling okay, although by the end I was exhausted and in a lot of pain,' says Márquez. He managed to get away from Pedrosa and engineer a one on one with Lorenzo for the last lap.

The last lap came and Lorenzo, who was winning comfortably, made a mistake; Márquez, who'd been waiting for it, passed him. Lorenzo refused to accept the humiliation and gave it everything, everything, on the last corner. 'He touched me, we touched, but it was great overtaking from Jorge, epic. And yes, I remembered Jerez: the last lap, the last corner, the possibility of passing, and with it taking victory – it's only logical he went for it. He went for it and he beat me. He beat me good.' So good that in the paddock afterwards, before getting up on the podium, Lorenzo came over to Márquez – echoes of Jerez – and apologised. 'Did I touch you?' the Majorcan asked Marc in Catalan. 'Yes, you did, but it was nothing, nothing – it was sweet, man, sweet!'

This is typical of Marc Márquez: big-hearted, generous, sincere, decent. As Valentino Rossi would say: 'Marc doesn't even entertain the idea of protesting; if he can, he'll overtake you back and that's the end of it.' Marc knew he'd managed more than could be expected that day, given that he was injured. And he knew, as a rider, that Lorenzo had overtaken in a manner that was on the limit, but fair. And that he hadn't been able to fight back because, firstly, he was up against an outstanding rival and, secondly, his shoulder was in no state for such shenanigans.

This side of Marc inspires admiration in everyone, beginning with those who deal with him on a daily basis. 'The press loves Marc,' explains Britain's Rhys Edwards, Head of Communications at Repsol Honda. 'He's the MotoGP golden boy, the media favourite, the fans' favourite. He has that common touch and he's captivating with it, just like Vale. Journalists feel comfortable with Marc, and Marc makes sure they do, even if he's not really in the mood. Marc always keeps smiling, come what may. The lad simply never disappoints, never. Everyone wants to talk to him, interview him, take photos … and Marc finds time for all of them, and especially for children. I've never known whether everything about him is natural or whether it's part of the job, part of his professionalism. I don't know and I don't care; all I know is that he's fantastic to work with because he always strikes the right balance.'

The championship moved on to the San Marino Grand Prix, at Misano, a circuit that has come to be known as 'Rossi's Garden': situated on the bustling Adriatic coast, it is a stone's throw away from The Doctor's home

'The press loves Marc. [...] He's the MotoGP golden boy [...] Marc always keeps smiling, come what may. The lad simply never disappoints, never.'

Rhys Edwards
Chief Press Officer at Repsol Honda

town. It proved to be another grand prix where Márquez was critical of his own performance, this despite managing his 12th podium place in 13 races and spending the entire weekend among the leaders. 'I can't be happy about a race in which – once again – I got off to a bad start, and then on the fourth turn, when I needed to close the gap, I went wide and lost even more time and ground,' says Márquez, who saw Lorenzo escape and leave the two Honda riders to fight it out for second place.

Yet that battle between team-mates was truly spectacular, and once again it nearly led to one rider, or indeed both riders, coming off. 'First of all I passed Dani,' recalls Márquez, 'then Dani passed me, with a move that was firm but fair. After that, more of the same. There was a little contact towards the end, but it was more of a friendly pat than anything else.' Márquez and Pedrosa talked about it before climbing on the podium, a conversation that

Previous pages: Marc likes to keep everyone happy. In these four images, we see him posing for a crowd of photographers in Qatar at the first grand prix of the season; letting himself be photographed by fans waiting at the door to his pit enclosure; kissing the camera after taking second place in Sepang; and walking through the press room at the Malaysian circuit, to take part in the podium finishers' press conference.

Dusk at Cheste. It's the last grand prix of the season, in Valencia, where Marc will be racing for the title. At the door to his pit enclosure, on Friday afternoon, he meets supporters who have been waiting for hours to see him. Marc never says 'no' to his fans.

was respectful if not quite as entertaining as Marc's 'Sweet, man, sweet!' exchange with Lorenzo at Silverstone.

Márquez finished the race with a sour taste in his mouth, stewing over the two mistakes he'd made towards the beginning of the race. Nakamoto, who misses nothing, also realised Marc was having trouble at the start line. 'What's going wrong at the start line, Marc?' the head of the racing team asked his rider. 'Boss, we have to do something about it for next year, we have to improve the clutch control because I still haven't got the hang of it and it's been a pain all season,' replied Márquez. 'We'll look into it,' was all Nakamoto would say.

The fact is, the relationship between Nakamoto and Márquez has been vital, a fundamental factor in Marc's explosion on to the MotoGP scene. Rarely have two people worked as well together as the Japanese engineer, responsible for Honda's performance at the World Championship, and the Catalan rider, the best rookie in history. It's a fluid relationship, affectionate, smiley, genuine, familiar and, above all, sincere. 'Me and Nakamoto don't talk about motorbikes,' Márquez points out. The rider has been known to greet his boss by pinching him on the leg, if Nakamoto has his back turned and hasn't noticed Marc enter the pit. 'There are many good things about Nakamoto, not least that he strives for perfection and always wants to win – always. You see? We're really quite alike,' adds Márquez.

'Obviously, this being his first year in MotoGP, Marc has made mistakes – who hasn't?! But luckily, the majority of his errors have been in training and not in races,' says Nakamoto. 'Our bike isn't easy to ride. All our riders, with the exception of Marc, have needed a year to adapt, a year's apprenticeship before they understand our machine, before they become assimilated to how it needs to be ridden and how to get the most out of it. But Marc was able to read it from day one, and exploit all its qualities in his debut season, and that's why he ended up as champion.'

According to the Honda chief, Marc has a number of qualities that make him an exceptional rider. 'Marc hasn't just been fast in learning about our bike and how it should be ridden, he also understood the tyres in a matter of months, something most professional riders take a long time to work out. Understanding how the wheels behave is vital when it comes to chasing victory in the last laps, which is when the podium places tend to

'All our riders [...] have needed a year to adapt [...] before they understand our machine [...] But Marc was able to read it from day one [...] and that's why he ended up as champion.'

Shuhei Nakamoto
Vice President of HRC

'It's not that we're friends exactly, but I'm the sort of person who believes that if someone's relaxed they can focus more and perform better. That's why I joke around with him, to keep him relaxed and help him stay focused. We're both big jokers.'

Shuhei Nakamoto
Vice President of HRC

Keeping the boss happy. Shuhei Nakamoto, who says he has an extraordinary relationship with Marc, shares a joke with the rider, top left; congratulates him in the paddock, top right; smiles on the first day Marc climbs aboard his new Honda at Cheste (November 2012), bottom left; celebrates the title win in Valencia with Julià, Marc's father, bottom right.

get decided.' Another virtue for Nakamoto is that 'Marc has the best reflexes I've ever seen in my life, and it's because of those reflexes that he can make decisions in thousandths of a second. The way he avoided a collision in Mugello, the speed and skill with which he acted, at 175mph with a wall approaching, is exactly what I'm talking about.' The Honda boss says of their relationship: 'It's not that we're friends exactly, but I'm the sort of person who believes that if someone's relaxed they can focus more and perform better. That's why I joke around with him, to keep him relaxed and help him stay focused. We're both big jokers.'

Before the World Championship heads off to Malaysia, Australia and Japan, with three races in as many weeks, there is another stop-off in Spain. At Motorland (Aragón) another show of power from Márquez sees him take pole, ten thousandths of a second ahead of Lorenzo. But in the race itself, one of the most bizarre accidents ever seen on a circuit takes place: the slightest of touches – practically non-existent – between Márquez and Pedrosa causes damage to the latter's traction control cable; as soon as Pedrosa tries to accelerate out of a corner, the bike flips violently and throws him on to the tarmac.

'It was a combination of factors, but really just a piece of terrible bad luck that has no explanation,' says Márquez, who has watched footage of the incident 1,000 times – 'or maybe 2,000'. Coming into a corner, Márquez almost piles into Pedrosa, but avoids doing so, before pulling away and taking off safely. Or so we think. On closer inspection, when the team-mates come together, with Dani slightly in front, there is contact not with Marc's left elbow, as it appeared, but with his clutch lever, which inserts itself inside the loop of Dani's traction control cable; when Márquez straightens his bike up, the lever pulls the cable away, snapping it and turning Dani's bike into a runaway horse.

The bad luck Márquez refers to is multiple: there was absolutely no intention on his part to cause an accident; the cable had a ridiculously large loop, big enough for the end of the clutch lever to fit inside; the cable was unprotected; and the security system failed to activate in time to prevent the motor from sending hundreds of units of horsepower to Pedrosa's rear wheel.

'When I reached the paddock as winner, before the television interviews, Suppo told me what had happened,' Márquez recalls. 'I said that's crazy –

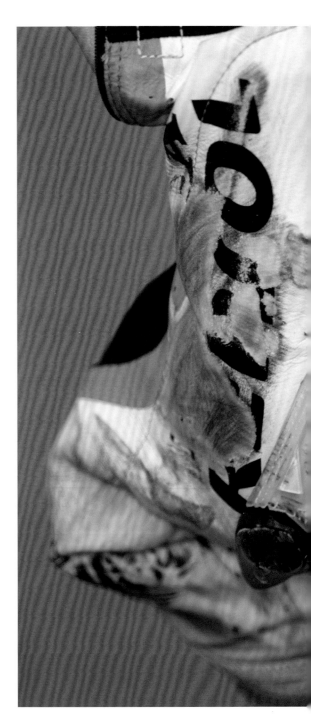

how could such a thing happen?' But, as he points out, because the incident involved two riders from the same team, they were able to find out exactly what had occurred. 'Dani's swing arm had a light black mark on it from my lever, and my lever had a light silver scratch on it from his swing arm. And on the telemetry we saw how my clutch activated the exact moment his cable snapped,' Márquez explains, still shocked at having inadvertently caused such an accident.

After showering, Márquez went to find Pedrosa, who accepted his apologies, but still reprimanded him for having come too close. 'Everyone agreed that the accident, though it was far more damaging to Dani, who could have challenged for the title right until the end, was the result of a series of misfortunes,' says Suppo. 'It was never Marc's intention to cause an accident, quite the opposite in fact, for as soon as he saw they were coming together he moved to the outside of the bend to avoid the crash, to avoid making contact with Dani.'

Despite all this, the accident reopened the debate about Márquez's riding style, not least because Race Direction announced that the incident was under investigation, and that it would take them two weeks to reach a verdict and decide whether Marc would be sanctioned, by which time the World Championship would have moved on to Malaysia. 'Marc has been too aggressive,' Pedrosa said. 'He needs to calm down instead of jumping the gun. It was only the sixth lap. Marc needs to understand that he's not the only one out there racing. It's very easy to race the way Marc races.' Lorenzo naturally joined in with the criticism: 'I still think Marc, very often, takes too many risks. But that's his style, perhaps he'll learn and calm down.'

It hurt Alzamora to hear the riding style of his star pupil criticised in this way, and he felt the incident was being blown out of all proportion. 'Established riders don't like a newcomer, a young lad, a novice, a rookie, just 20 years old, getting on their rear wheels, following them, refusing to be shaken off, and then passing them,' he says. 'And with Marc, not only was this happening, but after a few more races, other riders were finding it hard to follow him. This is obviously not a nice thing for established riders to have to swallow.' According to Alzamora, the essence of motorcycling is this: 'Young riders come along with ambition, with quality, with daring, trying to beat the established riders. It's the law of life. It's great that young riders try to throw them off their perch. Without such a mentality, it would be impossible to become champion. Obviously some riders don't like being pushed out of the spotlights.' Alzamora would later add that 'opinion over Marc's riding style changed as the season went by, until by the end you saw Lorenzo, who started out complaining about the way Marc rode, racing in desperation and performing some very questionable manoeuvres'.

At around this point, probably hoping to defuse the situation and protect his young disciple, or quite simply because he didn't think Marc's behaviour was worthy of sanction, Valentino Rossi waded into the argument, sarcastically demanding that Márquez be penalised 'for two or three years – yes, I'd stop him from riding for two or three years'. Rossi's view of Marc remained full of admiration. 'Marc's way of riding is his strength. Being aggressive is part of his style. It's nice to take on riders as committed as Marc, they make races much more fun and entertaining. I like Márquez as a person and I like him as a rider. He has the courage you need in world racing and he has race spirit. And I'm convinced he has the potential to become the best rider in history. Yes, even better than me.' By the end of the season, even Lorenzo shared this opinion: 'Marc is a phenomenon, the biggest phenomenon to hit MotoGP in the last 10 years. We both deserved the title, but he, as a rookie, perhaps deserved it that little bit more. He is definitely a worthy champion.'

The conclusion to that controversy – which, looking back, was clearly overblown – is that almost all Marc's racing colleagues ended up praising his committed riding, his determination and the courage highlighted by Rossi. Those were precisely the qualities that had struck Carmelo Ezpeleta, head of the World Championship organisation, three years earlier.

'To be honest, it was one of the most amazing sporting moments I've ever experienced, something that truly left me lost for words. It took place at Estoril in 2010, and the way Marc handled what was a very significant moment, a difficult and negative moment for him, was amazing. He was competing for the 125cc title; he fell off, wrecked the bike, took it to his pit to be repaired, waited while they put it back together again, then went back out and fought desperately to win. And he won, oh yes, he won,' remembers Ezpeleta, emotion showing in his voice. 'His exploits in 2013 were those of a master, but for me, that moment in Estoril, the way he got up and carried

'Established riders don't like a newcomer, a young lad [...] getting on their rear wheels, following them, refusing to be shaken off, and then passing them.'

Emilio Alzamora
Manager and former
125cc world champion

Carmelo Ezpeleta chats to Marc, as Emilio Alzamora looks on, in the Spanish Embassy in Tokyo a few days before the 2013 Japanese Grand Prix.

'He is simply the sort of young athlete who knows no boundaries. He's a guy who fights for himself and his people.'

Carmelo Ezpeleta
CEO of Dorna

on, was truly spectacular, and is the single thing that has most caught my eye about the lad. To act with that level of determination, you have to see things very clearly, you have to have courage, coolness and great strength in facing up to adversity.'

Ezpeleta had previously been coach and manager of the world champion rally driver Carlos Sainz. 'Marc reminds me a lot of the way Carlos was at the beginning,' says Ezpeleta. 'Like Carlos early on, Marc pays everyone a lot attention, he asks you things, looks like he's listening, and really is listening. I don't know, but I get the feeling that he is very attentive to what you tell him, but that afterwards, having compared what you've said to what countless other people have said to him, and his own ideas of course, he does whatever he wants, whatever he believes best suits his interests. And he's right. I don't know if he takes on board everything or just part of what you explain to him, but you finish the conversation feeling you've somehow contributed to his thinking, his decision making, and that's gratifying. Marc asks you for your opinion as part of his decision-making process.'

Ezpeleta is full of praise for the way Márquez conducted himself in negotiating the tough and tricky terrain of MotoGP in his first year. He hails Marc's hard-headed determination at each and every one of the riders' meetings, held on the Friday before every grand prix, where they discuss problems affecting the riders, the races, the category, the sport. 'Marc never shrinks, not even on his first day; he always makes sure his opinion is taken into account. And as he went on winning races and proving himself to be a tremendous competitor, his colleagues sat up and listened to what he had to say, took his opinions on board.'

'As far as I'm concerned, Marc is an outstanding athlete, exceptional, brilliant, a genuine pleasure to have among us,' Ezpeleta continues. 'He is simply the sort of young athlete who knows no boundaries. He's a guy who fights for himself and his people, someone prepared to battle to reach his goals and entertain the public. I agree that his charisma, his sunny disposition and his smile are all great and noteworthy, but what I like most about Marc is the way he races, the way he rides, and – I repeat – his determination.'

Ezpeleta reckons Márquez's aggressive and original riding style has had a huge influence, actually causing most of his rivals to change the way they ride. 'Nobody, nobody used to brake by blocking the front wheel, which Marc came up with, not worrying that the rear wheel ends up in the air. It's a devilish, brutal way of riding. And now everyone does it. Why? Because a kid comes along and does it. And, yes, it's doable. And, yes, braking like that, you win. There's no question Marc has created a school of riding.'

Márquez, Hernández, Alzamora, Nakamoto, Suppo, Honda and Repsol approached the Asian leg of the World Championship (Malaysia, Australia and Japan) with the aim of securing the title before returning home, to Valencia, for the last race of the season. Before starting practice in Sepang, Malaysia, Honda was sanctioned severely for not properly protecting the traction control cable on its RC213V and Márquez was penalised one point on his driver's licence. 'They sanctioned me because, with all the fuss that was made, they had to do something.'

Some people still remember Lorenzo sarcastically commenting that Márquez should have been rewarded rather than sanctioned, because, after all, 'What the public want to see is a spectacle.' Lorenzo went on, speaking in a serious tone, though his voice was thick with irony: 'I hated seeing

Dani go flying off his bike, but that's what the public want, that's what they buy. It's like the Roman amphitheatres, when the public demanded their sportsmen kill one another. Obviously these days people don't want us to kill each other, but when there are falls and the bikes touch, they buy the product more. We're modern-day gladiators. If we get hurt and have to stop racing, never mind.'

'Those comments were great for us,' Márquez points out. 'Dani and I began that grand prix with all eyes on us, but after Lorenzo's comments, attention moved elsewhere.' The race boiled down to another showdown between Jorge and Marc, with the youngster prevailing, behind Pedrosa. 'I took on Jorge in very confrontational fashion. We touched two or three times, but it was a fair and honourable fight,' Márquez recalls, happy to make do with 20 points for second place, 4 more than Jorge gained for coming third. 'Another grand prix ticked off, and with the points difference growing.'

Nothing suggested the next two fixtures, Phillip Island (Australia) and Motegi (Japan), would turn out like they did: descending into total chaos and uncertainty. In Australia, the tyres melted after 10 laps – in fact it would be more accurate to say they totally disintegrated after 10 laps, with holes you could fit your fist in. In Japan, dramatic weather conditions, including an earthquake, reduced the weekend's racing to a lottery. At Phillip Island, Race Direction was constantly changing its mind – not day to day, but hour to hour – over what the conditions and rules of the race would be. In the end, they decided to run the race in two legs, with the riders having to change bikes halfway, after 9 or 10 laps. Márquez's team got their sums wrong: Marc came in on lap 11 and was disqualified. Lorenzo took victory, and the World Championship was wide open again.

'It was a terrible error. We'd understood that you could complete lap 10 and come in to change bikes on lap 11,' recalls Hernández, for whom the incident is still a painful memory, even though Márquez went on to be crowned champion. 'If you can't count to 10, you become the laughing stock of the entire paddock, and you end up agonising about how it's possible to make such a childish error.' Luckily for the team and for Hernández, Márquez took control of the situation – Marc at his smiling and consoling best.

'The first thing I did was tell them that I make mistakes too, and I reminded them of my fall in Mugello – losing 20 precious points when

I was in second place,' says Márquez. 'I told them this because that's the way I feel, that we win and lose together. So we went out for dinner and then we went out to party. And we partied good. I knew it was a bit inappropriate, but I also knew it was the best way for us to move forward, to get the incident forgotten about as soon as possible, so as to focus on the Japan GP.' And it worked: as Márquez says, 'No one mentioned Australia again until Valencia.'

'What happened in Australia only reinforced our impression that with Marc we had someone very special, someone who knew how to lead at a very delicate moment. He took responsibility for getting that page turned as soon as possible,' remarks Suppo. 'Any other rider would have been furious for days, weeks, months even. Marc didn't just take charge of the situation, he spent the entire night encouraging the whole team. The manner in which he faced up to that disaster enabled us to approach the final two races in a way that guaranteed success, ensuring we won the title.' Suppo believes that 'if Marc had gone into the last two World Championship rounds full of

> 'What happened in Australia only reinforced our impression that with Marc we had someone very special, someone who knew how to lead at a very delicate moment. [...] Marc didn't just take charge of the situation, he spent the entire night encouraging the whole team.'
>
> *Livio Suppo*
> *Repsol Honda Team Manager*

Marc tries to recover his bike after coming off in testing at Phillip Island.

The jump. Having been told the Australian Grand Prix will be run in two stages, Marc and his team practise changing bikes, as seen in this sequence of images.

A delighted Shuhei Nakamoto congratulates Marc on taking second place in Japan.

resentment, he certainly wouldn't have won the title, because when there's resentment, anger and tension, nobody does a good job. Everything turned out wonderfully, thanks to Marc's smile and optimism.'

Before flying from Australia to Japan, people kept asking Márquez what his hopes were for the next race: 'All I ask is that it's a normal grand prix,' he replied. But that weekend in Motegi proved to be one of the worst weekends of the century. It didn't just rain, it was dangerously windy; there was a tsunami and even an earthquake, enough to make the buildings shake. On the circuit, nobody talked of anything else. Meanwhile, Race Direction made emergency plans, organising qualifying at the last minute on Saturday, and more free practice than usual on the Sunday morning.

To make a further mockery of his own request for a 'normal grand prix', Márquez hit the deck in practice just before the start. Falling on the wet track could have robbed him of any chance of being crowned champion. 'I thought I'd seriously hurt myself, but luckily it was no more than a hard blow to the back. They gave me a pain-killing injection and I could go out and race.' The race turned out to be a pursuit of Lorenzo, at the end of which Márquez had to make do with a valiant second place (20 more points), with a cautious Pedrosa at his back.

But there was great joy for Marc that weekend. Dressed in his race suit, he watched Àlex win the Moto3 race, the first grand prix victory of his brother's career, thanks to a masterful last lap. 'A last lap we'd planned together, because I knew, on a track full of corners, that Àlex had it in him to beat the rest of the field and take the race, and so it proved. Seeing your brother perform a last lap exactly as you planned it with him – down to the last millimetre – that's an indescribable feeling.'

This is because Marc's little brother is much more than just a little brother. As mother Roser explains, 'Now that they're both grown up, they've

Brotherhood. Marc, dressed in his race suit ready for MotoGP action at Motegi, congratulates his brother, Àlex, on winning the Moto3 race.

started sharing many more things than they used to, very specifically, of course, their professions: their preparation, making sure everything turns out as well as possible for each of them, their instinct to try and better themselves every single day, and, above all, their outlook on life, always trying to make life pleasant for others, never holding back on a smile.' For Àlex is just as much of a joker as his brother: you have to like joking around to get on with the Márquez brothers!

They are not just brothers but the closest of friends. 'None of us really have that many friends, do we? Because it's one thing to know a person, to share things and interact with someone, and it's quite another thing, a very different thing, to have a person as a friend,' says Marc, regarding his special relationship with his brother. 'My best friend is called Edgar, and he's three years older than me. I also have a great relationship with Gerard Piqué, the footballer, with whom I've had lots of fun times, and I still have one or two schoolmates, but that's about it.' Girlfriend? 'No, I don't have a girlfriend, and it's going to be hard for me to have one because of the life I lead, the

'Now that they're both grown up, they've started sharing many more things [...] above all, their outlook on life, always trying to make life pleasant for others, never holding back on a smile.'

Roser Alentà
Àlex and Marc's mother

Courtesy of Repsol Media/Jaime Olivares.

Friends. Marc is congratulated by his friend Gerard Piqué, the footballer, at the Valencia Grand Prix, where Marc sealed the MotoGP World Championship.

job I do. I had a great relationship with a girl for a few years, but we gave it up last summer because it was impossible to maintain a regular, stable relationship. Essentially, as I said, because of my travelling, my timetable, my training, my commitments and all the rest of it, it's really very hard.'

But back to Àlex's victory in that amazing last lap – a very 'Márquez' victory, it's worth reiterating – which must have had Grandad Ramon leaping in the air back in Cervera, and caused mayhem in the Estrella Galicia team pit, from where Julià watched the heroic achievement. 'It was lovely to see Àlex, who has fought very hard for his first victory, get his brother's congratulations. As a father you feel proud for having created a good atmosphere at home, brotherly rivalry and occasional bickering aside – a home where they spend a good part of their lives together. They do everything together, always with smiles on their faces.'

'They've always been very close,' says Roser, their mother. 'They're both passionate about their work and provide each other with mutual support, and to us as parents this is obviously very gratifying.'

More than just brothers. Àlex and Marc spend their lives together. They live with their parents in Cervera, train together and compete at the same grand prix meetings. They share each other's joys and disappointments – and often share a scooter to and from the paddock.

'I've always admired how clearly he sees things.'

Àlex Márquez
Marc's brother and a Moto3 rider

Cheste: the Finale

The whole family travelled to Cheste (Valencia) together, including Uncle Ramon, president and manager of his nephews' fan clubs. This time Marc decided to put all other activities on hold for the weekend. 'I know it's not the done thing, but people have to understand that I need to concentrate on the task in hand,' he explained to his inner circle. That whole weekend he was going back and forth between his trailer and the pit, concentrating on his work, then spending the evenings with his family. 'It was the most important race of my life and I just couldn't mess it up, so I created a bubble – trailer-to-pit, pit-to-trailer – and made myself available to nobody.'

It's said that the meeting Hernández called on the Thursday afternoon was quite a strange one. Marc's head coach and another mechanic thanked Márquez for the season, saying what a pleasure it had been and trying to tactfully let him know that, come what may, whether they ended up as champions or not, it had been an enjoyable year's racing; that what had already been achieved, and the manner in which it had been achieved, was reward enough. They were essentially saying what a pleasure it had been working with him. 'We don't know how this will end, but don't worry, you've ridden a great championship,' they told him.

'But what are you saying?' Márquez replied. 'Are you saying that it doesn't matter if we don't win the title because it wasn't in our plans? Are you honestly saying that to me? Really? Come on, guys, come on, we're here to win! We have to finish off the job we started almost a year ago, on this very circuit, on what was a dog of a day. What happened in Australia can only be put right by winning the title on Sunday,' he added bluntly. 'Don't give me that rubbish that we can be satisfied with what we've achieved so far. No way! You guys want this too, you guys deserve this title too – or am I wrong?' He wasn't wrong.

Marc was equally assured on the track, where he was spectacular all weekend. He started off by securing a magnificent pole, with Lorenzo almost half a second back, showing that if he didn't challenge for the win on Sunday, it was because he didn't need to. Nevertheless, before the race, Nakamoto met with Márquez alone and asked him for a favour, practically begged him in fact. 'Marc, you've already taken plenty of risks this season, wouldn't you say? You've fallen a lot. True, almost always in training, but

today you're going to do me a favour: think of me, think of my heart, do it for me, please, and remember that what we want out of today is the title.'

Livio Suppo was maybe thinking the same thing at the same time. 'I've never raced on tarmac, so I have no way of really knowing what's risky and what's not,' says Suppo, but nevertheless he too was thinking that this race, Valencia, the last grand prix of the season, was no place for taking risks or doing anything silly. 'Naturally, though, from my point of view, the difference between being spectacular and being aggressive is a very fine line – minuscule, you might say.' Having reached the final stage of the World Championship, Suppo was of the opinion – and rightly so – that 'the most emotional moments, the most spectacular moves of the MotoGP season, had already been performed. And mostly by Marc, in one sense or another, which is something of great merit, because it's a way of life, a way of riding, a mental outlook. Marc doesn't just want to win, he wants to win entertainingly. There are those who think only of winning, and that's fine, but I prefer those who think about entertaining too, because they make our sport grow.' In conclusion, Suppo says, 'Of course the entertainers are the ones who take more risks, but if you weigh up the pros and cons, those who win without entertaining don't give the sport any colour.'

Márquez says his mind was already set and he planned to take only the most minimal risks; that having reached Cheste, entertainment would come from being crowned champion, not by offering the most beautiful, emotional and spectacular race of the season. 'I was convinced – and was right, as it turned out – that Jorge would try and slow the race down and cause some sort of mix-up, the more riders involved the better,' says Márquez. It was also clear to Marc that it was unlikely that either Crutchlow – who is particularly fond of Marc – or Bautista, a fellow Honda rider, or Bradl, who also rides for the same manufacturer, would try and make life difficult for their colleague. Which left Jorge, Dani and Valentino … and Márquez could finish fourth and win the championship.

Nevertheless, the early part of the race was certainly hair-raising, with a group of riders bunched together at the front, riding around Scalextric-style, with huge potential for mishap. 'Jorge, who'd been critical of my style all year, tried to make it difficult, constantly changing his line, braking at the wrong time, making a mess, causing chaos,' Marc recalls. 'I feared the worst: I knew any one of us could move a fraction too soon or take the wrong line and cause a pile-up. I thought Dani would escape and force Jorge to chase after him, but that never happened.'

Halfway through the race, as the group started to stretch out, Lorenzo looked behind him and saw that only Dani and Marc were still with him and that Valentino was already a long way behind, giving the impression that he wasn't keen to create problems either. 'I decided to take off and go for victory, my eighth of the season – not too bad,' Lorenzo recalls. 'I tried to make life difficult for Marc, of course I did, but he'd had a great year and it was very hard to imagine him making a mistake and running into trouble. He was a very deserving champion.'

The most touching scene came courtesy of Santi Hernández – who else? – Marc's head coach, the man who had suffered most for the Phillip Island debacle, the gentleman who'd owned up and blamed himself for not being able to count to 10 properly. 'It was a never-ending final lap, absolute torment. I spent the whole lap staring at the bend that leads on to the finishing strait. When I finally saw Marc coming, I waited for him to bring the bike up, and when he had it upright I closed my eyes and put my head in my hands. I took myself away from everyone and everything, and didn't even see him cross the finishing line. I didn't need to. I didn't want to. I started crying with joy. I wanted a minute to myself, just for me. I know the first person to come and congratulate me was Livio. Then I looked for Emilio, and we cried like children together for a while. We deserved it, we most certainly did!'

It had been many, many years since a rider, a youngster, a rookie with a smile, had inspired such happiness, recognition and unanimous praise. He had become so popular, so quickly, that in a sense it was everyone's title – it seemed as if the whole world had been rooting for Marc Márquez Alentà to win the championship. Since Marc started in MotoGP, people had stopped asking, 'What time's the Moto Grand Prix?' or 'What time are the bikes on?' Now it was 'What time's Márquez on?' – just as it used to be 'What time's Rossi on?'

Clearly the support for Marc and the confidence shown in him by Repsol have been invaluable to the rider. At the same time the Spanish energy company has likewise been rewarded, and not just by Marc triumphing spectacularly in the premier class for the Repsol Honda MotoGP team. The Repsol–Márquez pairing, backed by Amilio Alzamora's input and strategy, works on many levels.

Teresa de Istúriz (Manager of Publicity, Marketing and Sponsorship at Repsol), Mila Vior (Deputy Manager of Public Relations and Sponsorship) and Beatriz Tobio (Chief of Sponsorship) are pictured posing together with Marc for a happy photo, the sponsor's joy combining with the champion rider's satisfaction. The three women agree that the association between

Márquez and Repsol has been hugely valuable to the company because Marc, besides being a great advert for their products (fuel and lubricant oil), contributes to the brand through his behaviour on and off the track, defending Repsol's values and principles.

'It's important to do things well, but it's also important how you do them,' explains Mila Vior. 'Marc does everything with a smile, with pleasure and great responsibility. Like Repsol, Marc is always trying to better himself, setting new goals as soon as he's achieved his existing ones.' Another important feature of Marc's personality, she says, 'is that he never tires, and if he suffers a mishap when chasing his dream, he doesn't lose hope, he keeps on trying until he gets there. Proof of this came in 2011, when he suffered an eye injury just as he was about to win the Moto2 title.'

Mila remembers , 'as if it were yesterday', the day she was first introduced to Marc, in 2008, when he was only 15. 'I was very impressed by him: he was only little, very young, very lively and alert, and really friendly. What most impressed me was the twinkle in his eye. As Teresa [de Istúriz] would say, those of us who live our lives and jobs passionately do have a twinkle in our eye. Marc was only 15, but even then he looked at you firmly, he didn't blink, and he paid you careful attention.' Mila goes on to explain how, even then, whenever any of them saw Marc, they'd say the same thing Grandad Ramon would always say: 'Be fast, but be careful.' And Marc would always reply in the same manner: 'Don't worry, I do this because I can, because it comes easy to me, even though, from the outside, it looks complicated to you.'

Like many people – although she has more reason than most, having witnessed Marc's growth as a person and a sportsman over a number of years – Mila considers the role the Márquez Alentà family has played in his development as being vital. 'Many people would love to have the sort of family Marc's got. Not only has he got a great family, he appreciates how lucky he is to have them. Obviously Marc has been born with a gift – or two, or even more – but without the support and sacrifice of Julià and Roser, and all his other people, he wouldn't be where he is today. Then you've also got everyone who has helped him: his team, his mechanics, his coaches, us at Repsol, everyone who has believed in him. Clearly we've all given a lot, but he's given it back with interest, and especially with that twinkle in his eye. Marc gives everyone energy, and to us at Repsol he brings youth, freshness,

'I was very impressed by him: he was only little, very young, very lively and alert, and really friendly. What most impressed me was the twinkle in his eye.'

Mila Vior
Deputy Manager for Repsol Public Relations and Sponsorship

After winning the US Grand Prix at Austin, Texas, Marc poses with Repsol Honda's Teresa de Istúriz, Mila Vior and Beatriz Tobio.

excitement, enthusiasm and happiness. And, I should add, strength and courage, because Marc always looks forward, always.'

Mila is convinced that whatever field he'd chosen as a child, Marc's great intelligence would have seen him succeed in it. Intelligence on a number of levels: listening, learning, asking for help when required, forming a team and always looking on the bright side of life. 'We also work as a team, and we admire the way he makes sure his team is his "other family", through his attitude, behaviour, the little winks, even the tricks he plays. And he's right to do this, absolutely right. That's why his victories are the product of collective hard work, why the excitement is shared throughout the team, his "other family".' Mila considers Marc to be a true leader, 'because a leader is not someone who ends up occupying high posts or having power, rather it's someone people follow because they believe in him. And that's Marc Márquez Alentà all over.'

It is no surprise that Mila imagines Marc would be a success in any role at Repsol: in Human Resources, 'because he's a born leader'; in Communications, 'because he's a great communicator, a pioneer in his field, an innovator'; even in Exploration, 'because of his courage, and even his riding style, which is revolutionary, distinct, unique, so he'd be able to overcome challenges and ensure a bright future'. Furthermore, everything Marc does bears his seal, his trademark, his style. 'You see, that's another of Marc's qualities: he loves what he does; he has fun with what he does and with how he does it, and this excitement and pleasure rubs off on others,' adds Mila.

One quality Alzamora has always highlighted in his pupil is his receptiveness: 'He's an absolute sponge, he absorbs everything he sees and hears around him.' Mila agrees: 'It's possible Marc has fed off every single one of us, but equally we've all learned a lot from him.' She adds: 'When we look at Marc, we see the values we try to highlight in our company, especially that spirit of constant self-improvement. In fact we were recently recalling, with our President, Antonio Brufau, the day in 2010, when Marc came to present us with the 125cc World Championship trophy, his first big title. I remember the President saying to him: "Don't forget, we'll always want you with us, by our side. I want to see you riding for us in MotoGP and I want to see you winning the title with us." And here we are today – he's the youngest champion in the history of the premier category, riding for our team, the Repsol Honda Team. It's been an enormous pleasure to be able to share this epic achievement with so many people, those who have followed him throughout his stunning career – a career which, we hope, has a lot of life in it yet.'

Even veterans of the press room, people who watched all the greats race – Kenny Roberts, Barry Sheene, Freddie Spencer, Eddie Lawson, Kevin Schwantz, Wayne Rainey, Wayne Gardner, Mick Doohan, Àlex Crivillé and Valentino Rossi – and became friends with many of them, are united in their verdict: Márquez is the best they've seen in years.

'Marc is a gift from heaven to this sport and to those of us who love racing.'

Jean-Claude Schertenleib
Swiss journalist on Le Matin

'Not even with Kenny Roberts, who revolutionised the racing world with his aggressive style, did we see anything similar,' the American journalist Dennis Noyes points out. 'Márquez has become the greatest in history at only 20 years of age. He dominated in 2013 and won, yes, on Honda circuits, but also on Yamaha ones. We are seeing a brilliant champion, and there's really no limit in terms of what he can achieve in his career.'

As far as Jean-Claude Schertenleib, Swiss journalist on *Le Matin*, is concerned, 'Marc is a gift from heaven to this sport and to those of us who love racing. Motorcycling will soon lose Rossi, and Márquez will be there to take up his mantle in everything, on and off the track.' Schertenleib believes that both Lorenzo and Pedrosa owe their improvement to Márquez. 'Marc is an outright threat to them and he's forced them to improve. He's inspired them. We have never seen Lorenzo as brilliant, as extraordinary, as he was when battling with Márquez for the MotoGP title.'

Matt Roberts, a former BBC journalist who has published a biography of the Australian rider Casey Stoner, is full of praise for 'the style with which Márquez, a rookie, a novice, has made the premier category his own. The speed with which he adapted was spectacular and he showed brutal mental strength, fearlessly taking on the big beasts in Rossi, Lorenzo and Pedrosa.' Like many people, Roberts considers the way Marc overcame his 175mph fall at Mugello, and dealt with the outrageous team mistake in Australia, 'as proof apparent that we're dealing with a great champion'.

For Gavin Emmett, another English reporter, 'Lorenzo and Pedrosa are Spanish riders, whereas Márquez is a world figure: he's been adopted by everyone. It's like with Rossi – he's a one-man World Heritage Site.' Emmett also believes 'the best is still to come, for there's nothing greater than seeing two wounded lions, like Jorge and Dani, having to react, knowing they'll have to raise their games if they don't want to keep being beaten by the *piccolo bastardo*, as Doctor Rossi affectionately calls him'.

Frenchman Michel Turco, at *Moto Revue* magazine, says, 'the thing about Márquez's riding is that, while Lorenzo and Pedrosa suffer on their bikes, Marc enjoys himself like a man possessed'. Italy's Enrico Borghi, from *Moto Sprint* magazine, believes, 'Marc will define an era because he has the excitement, passion, character and courage that the greatest champions in history have always had.'

'Marc's capacity to learn is outrageous,' states Giovanni Zagmani, of Moto.it. 'To anyone who says Marc only wins because he rides a Honda, I'd remind them that last season was Pedrosa's eighth year on a Honda bike and he still hasn't been world champion.' Japan's Akira Nishimura, from the daily *Sportiva*, is convinced that 'we won't see a rider like Marc ever again; no one will come along, aged just 20, and teach us the things that boy taught us. There won't be another lad as brave and courageous as him.'

'It's hard to find words to describe what Márquez has achieved,' says Matthew Birt of *Motorcycle News*. 'He's going to dominate the World

'Lorenzo and Pedrosa are Spanish riders, whereas Márquez is a world figure: he's been adopted by everyone. It's like with Rossi – he's a one-man World Heritage Site.'

Gavin Emmett
English journalist

'[...] we won't see a rider like Marc ever again; no one will come along, aged just 20, and teach us the things that boy taught us. There won't be another lad as brave and courageous as him.'

Akira Nishimura
Japanese journalist from the daily Sportiva

Carlos Liñán welcomes his rider into the paddock at Austin's Circuit of the Americas after Marc's first MotoGP grand prix victory.

Championship the way Doohan and Rossi did. If it weren't for Lorenzo, Marc would have been champion with one arm tied behind his back.' 'Marc has nine lives, like a cat: he falls but never gets injured,' says the US rider Randy Mamola, four times world 500cc runner-up. He adds: 'Lorenzo and Pedrosa are only able to ride MotoGP one way, via one line; Marc goes wherever he wants, does whatever takes his fancy.' Carlo Pernat, manager of the Pramac Ducati team, goes further: 'This is the bike of a generation, a bike that has been waiting years for a rider to come along and understand it, to make it his own, to ride it the way it was conceived.'

Mick Doohan has a similar view: 'Marc was born to ride this bike; we should stop criticising his riding and just enjoy watching him on the track. If we've learned anything, it's that his spells in 125cc and Moto2 were mere steeping stones on the way to becoming the youngest senior class champion in history.' Lewis Hamilton, the Formula One driver now with Mercedes, caused a similar storm in his first season in the seniors, taking on the giants of the grid and shaking the whole sport up. He says: 'What Marc has done is almost surreal. Beating former and reigning champions when you're so young feels like being on a massive roller-coaster. You can't explain it, but you just carry on trying to do it over and over again. Marc just needs to make sure he enjoys the moment.'

'There are lots of things you can say about Marc,' states Ángel Nieto, the multiple Spanish motorcycling champion. 'You can talk about his character and his contagious smile, because he, like me, loves surrounding himself with people who enjoy their jobs, who enjoy what they do. But I would just say that he seems like a brilliant kid. You tend to see young lads who have got a certain something, who show great promise but don't make it for one reason or another. Marc has got it all and he's exploded on to the MotoGP scene in his debut season. Did I expect it? No, I can't say I did, at least not in such brilliant and crushing fashion. He has been cavalier, delightfully cavalier, unafraid of taking on, and beating, the champion riders.'

'This *ragazzino* has a big future ahead of him,' states Giacomo Agostini, sitting beside Nieto in the Yamaha pit at Mugello. 'He's got a certain charm and we'll never tire of enjoying his victories, because he's young and talented, he's got that special something about him, he's at Honda, and he's got his head screwed on.' Livio Suppo also emphasises Marc's coolness under pressure, recalling the obstacles he overcame to win the 125cc title. 'You only have to remember the incident at Estoril, on the very day he could have done without it; or how he lost his first title in Moto2, in Malaysia, suffering from that sudden eye injury. These things would have finished most people, and yet Marc picked himself up and ended up winning both titles. Obviously, without such a cool head it would be impossible to overcome difficult moments like that.'

Marc himself reckons that his cool head, like his smile, is part of his DNA: 'We have to start somewhere, so let's blame the parents.' But in his moment of triumph and joy he doesn't want to leave anybody out: he recalls the generous attention of the brothers Jordi and Josep Rojas; likewise Ángel Viladoms, Joan Moreta, Comercial Impala, the RACC, Guim Roda, Álvar Garriga, the Procurve team, Pío Ventura, his son Iván and – naturally – the Escola Monlau, Honda and Repsol. And Jaume Curco too, who's involved in all aspects of racing and is a patron of Motoclub Segre. It was Curco who once said to Alzamora: 'As soon as you get a chance, you have to go and see this lad from Cervera – you'll be amazed.'

Alzamora duly went to see him and ended up spellbound by a lad who was always beating boys who were older than him. Just as he does now with Valentino Rossi, Dani Pedrosa and Jorge Lorenzo. 'There were days,' says Ángel Viladoms, current President of the Spanish Federation of Motocycling, 'when he made the podium in every category he competed in: enduro, motorcross and speedway.' Viladoms likes to joke about the way Márquez, since childhood, has always had a special feel for motorbikes: 'He just senses how the bike is behaving, because he's blessed with an exceptional arse – he has a backside full of sensors!'

'There's more than one way of feeling that you're a rider,' explains Roda, who worked with Márquez when he was 11. 'One way is riding with verve, passion and courage; and another – without doubt the better way – is riding with a certain coldness, understanding what's happening to you on board the bike. Being daring will get you nowhere. Sure, once in a while it might afford you the odd victory and make you think you're the business, but in the long run you'll end up hurting yourself. Riding while understanding what's happening, working out the why of things, that's what lets you get the best out of yourself and the bike. And that's Marc all over.'

'[...] he seems like a brilliant kid. [...] He has been cavalier, delightfully cavalier, unafraid of taking on, and beating, the champion riders.'

Ángel Nieto
Multiple Spanish motorcycling champion

'This *ragazzino* has a big future ahead of him. He's got a certain charm [...] he's got that special something about him [...] and he's got his head screwed on.'

Giacomo Agostini
Fifteen-time world champion

During the pre-race ceremonies at the Qatar Grand Prix, Marc shares a joke with British rider Cal Crutchlow.

Garriga, who was Marc's mechanic from the age of 9 to 11, is of the opinion that 'the most amazing thing about Marc, what makes him unique, is the coolness with which he rides, his calm way of understanding risk and everything that's going on around him – which is plenty – while not letting difficulties effect him emotionally'. Roda, the 'maestro', concludes: 'When you learn to control your emotions, that's when you start to mature. It was that sense of maturity in Marc, even when still a child, that was so surprising, so amazing.'

'There's no duplicity with Marc. That smile – you can't fake it, you just can't,' says Ramon Royes, Mayor of Cervera. Roser Atienza, Marc's one-time schoolteacher, says, 'Even as a little boy, he had very clear ideas. He was never impulsive and you notice that on the track, because he makes decisions in milliseconds and is rarely wrong. He was already like that at school.' Marc's brother Àlex says, 'I've always admired how clearly he sees things.' But their mother, Roser, perhaps sums things up best: 'He doesn't swell when he wins or shrink when he loses; he always has his feet on the ground and a smile on his face.'

It's worth sitting down with Grandad Ramon and taking a look at his armchair. *Avi* was right all along: 'You can do anything, lad.' He was right, but given everything else that's happened – with Marc having produced the most spectacular debut season in history and gone on to dominate the following one – it's also fair to say Marc rather ignored Ramon's other piece of advice: 'And like I always say: be fast, but be careful.' Sure thing, Grandad, sure thing. To climb aboard that 'mule' takes a tonne of courage, courage Ramon's grandson has in spades. Meanwhile, Ramon ruins his armchair. He's given in to his son, Julià, and stopped setting off firecrackers. But he still swerves Doña Sole and stays up into the middle of the night. Watching his grandson race is better than any dream.

'[...] he's blessed with an exceptional arse – he has a backside full of sensors!'

Ángel Viladoms
President of the Spanish Federation of Motocycling

A few scratches. The seat of Marc's race suit, worn through from scraping the track, after the French Grand Prix at Le Mans.

Memories of a Dream Come True

The lad with the loose leg, the motorbike acrobat, the boy who asked Father Christmas for a 'racing' motorbike aged four, has seen his dreams come true year after year. It would seem Marc Márquez is built of the stuff dreams are made of.

There he is, taking his left foot off the bike as he comes into and speeds out of every turn, in the manner of racing legend Valentino Rossi – that is to say, in the manner of The Doctor and every other rider these days. Using feet as rudders is certainly one way of keeping the bike afloat while surfing the tarmac at over 200mph.

The images that follow recall how yet another dream has come true for Marc – the third and greatest of all.

Aeroplanes, hotels, hire cars ... living at close quarters. Such
is the life of a rider when travelling. But Marc's 'other family'
knows there will also be laughter and fun along the way.
Here's Marc sporting 'fashion' sunglasses at Austin, Texas,
and joking around in the hotel lift in Kuala Lumpur, Malaysia.

Travel sharing

It's not easy moving constantly from one place to another – from Europe to the USA, on to Malaysia, Australia and Japan, then back to the Mediterranean, to Valencia. Marc has his people and he makes sure they are always with him. Here he is with his team-mate Dani Pedrosa, preparing to cross a road in Doha, Qatar, and chatting with Carlos Liñán, his trusted mechanic, on the plane back from Sachsenring, after winning the German Grand Prix; and, on the next pages, dining out in Austin, Texas, with Gabriele Mazzarolo (owner of Alpinestars), and his managers at Repsol Honda, Livio Suppo and Shuhei Nakamoto.

Big day, historic day

Take a good look at these photographs. They might appear to be routine, insignificant even. They might even look like snapshots taken from a mobile phone. But they are none of these things. They are photos of a historic moment. Despite the untimely bad weather on that 13 November 2012 in Valencia, Marc christened his Honda RC213V. He's dressed in white – and in many ways their relationship will be like a marriage. He goes out and registers times that will astound even Livio Suppo, one of his team managers. After seeing Marc set a new record for the first section of the Cheste track, Suppo felt compelled to get his mobile out and take a photo of the screen showing the times. 'It was unbelievable what he'd just done! Unprecedented!' So everything started here. That's why there is such a look of concentration on Marc's face in the next few images, as he climbs a wall to get a look at his new rivals, and as he walks through the paddock at the Valencia circuit.

Always with a sense of humour. As Shuhei Nakamoto says, 'Marc and I both love joking around, it helps keep us focused.' This is how Marc lives and competes. Here you have him dodging Mirco Lazzari's lens in the press room at Phillip Island, Australia, after a grand prix to forget, or learn from; and above, posing with a supporter outside the door of the Repsol Honda enclosure in Sepang, Malaysia.

The man of the moment in MotoGP

Rhys Edwards, Repsol Honda's Communications Manager, describes Marc as 'the golden boy of MotoGP'. One of the reasons Marc is the man of the moment is because he never says 'no' to anyone. And because he has a captivating smile. And because he loves interacting with his fans, with his supporters, with the public in general. And because he's grateful for the life he leads. Here he can be seen crouching down, almost on his knees, to autograph a shirt. On the following pages, a group of supporters in the stands at Sepang, dozens of fans waiting for an autograph at Cheste, and Marc taking selfies with more fans at Motorland, Aragón, where he posed over and over again, with anyone who asked him to.

Life, study and racing, in 18 different corners of the world

Some places are more appealing than others. Some circuits are more attractive than others. Yet Marc's life is the same everywhere: work hard on Thursday, Friday and Saturday, to give himself a chance of winning on Sunday. 'We don't strive to make newspaper headlines, or to be the star turn on Friday or Saturday; we work in order to give Marc as well prepared a motorbike as possible on Sunday,' says Santi Hernández, his head coach. And Marc, seen here in his office in Brno, Czech Republic, and below in his trailer in Sepang, Malaysia, never stops studying. In the next few images, we see him entering the pit in Phillip Island, Australia, and coming out of the workshop in Valencia, at the grand prix where he became the youngest MotoGP champion in history.

Andrea 'Mondo' Brunetti collects Marc's Honda (93) after his victory in Indianapolis, followed by Dani Pedrosa's mechanic (Pedrosa finished second). On the right, Belgium's Roger van der Borght, a Repsol Honda team coordinator, takes Marc's bike away after a fall in Assen (The Netherlands).

On the left, Marc, focused, seconds before going out for training at Jerez and at Assen. On the right, riding out of the pit at Silverstone, where he finished second in the British Grand Prix, behind Jorge Lorenzo (Yamaha) and ahead of Dani Pedrosa (Honda).

It's not easy controlling the enormous power – truly enormous, though the riders always want more – of a MotoGP bike. This can be seen in these two images, taken on the same lap at Sachsenring (Germany), where Marc won ahead of Britain's Cal Crutchlow (Tech 3 Yamaha) and Italy's Valentino Rossi (Yamaha), in the absence of Jorge Lorenzo (Yamaha) and Dani Pedrosa (Honda).

Above, the tension seen in Marc's arms, the hands gripping the handlebars hard and the right knee sticking out show that Marc is in control of the bike, but his rear wheel is dangerously off the ground. To the right, Marc enters the turn at a tilt.

Life at the track

Marc lives in hotels or 'trailers', but he spends his day in the vast circuit enclosure, a trackside apartment, with views of the tarmac. Here Marc can be seen among his people. On the right, he smiles as he listens to his telemetry expert, Carlo Liuzzi. In the main image, he sits beside Santi Hernández, his coach, and Giulio Nava, his other telemetry analyst, while Roberto Clerici watches on. In the next pages, he is seen in the pit at Silverstone (Great Britain), and striding through the pit enclosure in Qatar, all around him a blur.

On course to his fourth victory

It's often said that life is lived in colour but photos should be in black and white. This photograph by Mirco Lazzari illustrates why: the contrast between the absolute black and the transparent white, with all shades of grey in between, conveys a sense of destiny – it's as if Marc, as he walks out of the door and into the pit at Indianapolis, knows he's going to win the race, knows he's going to achieve his fourth victory of the season, again finishing ahead of Dani Pedrosa (Honda) and Jorge Lorenzo (Yamaha).

Marc walks down the home straight of
the Losail circuit in Qatar, heading for the
finishing line where he will pose with his
premier category colleagues for the season's
official photograph.

Above, Marc poses at the circuit in Assen, Netherlands. Right, he blows kisses to the crowd during the MotoGP riders parade, on the morning of the Australian Grand Prix at Phillip Island.

Marc heads back to the pit enclosure after posing for photos with fans at Motegi, Japan. Right, he rides through the paddock at Silverstone on his way to the podium, after finishing second, behind Jorge Lorenzo (Yamaha) and ahead of Dani Pedrosa (Honda).

As soon as the lights change

On your marks, get set, go! This is not just any moment. The lights go out, the track lights up; absolute silence becomes a stampede of runaway horses. Getting off to a good start is crucial. Or at least it is for most riders: Marc recognised it was one of his weaknesses, an area he needed to improve. Because of this, the first few laps too often become a bit of a roller-coaster ride for Marc.

Left, the start at Austin, Texas, where Marc made history by winning his first MotoGP. Above, the start at Laguna Seca, another US Grand Prix and another historic day, which saw Marc passing Valentino Rossi on the famous Corkscrew.

On the following pages, the start at Qatar, where Marc lived up to the prediction made by Shuhei Nakamoto six months earlier ('Marc will make the podium in his first GP') by finishing third; and a spectacular shot of the start of the San Marino Grand Prix at Misano, front wheels in the air.

Austin, scene of the first great record

When Marc says dreams can come true, he perhaps has this image in mind: the first lap of the Circuit of The Americas at Austin, Texas, and his first real chance of winning a premier category grand prix. Indeed, it proved to be his first triumph, a date with destiny. Furthermore, he managed it from start to finish, leading from Thursday to Sunday, totally in control of proceedings at all times.

The image is also indicative of how the season will play out. Dani Pedrosa (Honda, 26, on the left) escaped with Marc (93), with Jorge Lorenzo (Yamaha, 99) just behind them. Shortly after the halfway stage, Marc picked up the pace, overtook his team-mate and started making history as the youngest rider ever to win a GP in the senior class, aged 20 years and 63 days (already being the youngest winner of a Moto2 race), beating Freddie Spencer's record (20 years and 98 days) set in Argentina in 1982.

Two lovely scenes, ballet dancing on tarmac. On the left, Marc takes a chicane at Austin, ahead of two Ducati riders, the USA's Nicky Hayden and Italy's Andrea Dovizioso. The next image speaks volumes: Marc is chased by Jorge Lorenzo (Yamaha) and Dani Pedrosa (Honda), a snapshot of the World Championship itself.

A brilliant panorama of the most spectacular
sloping corner on the calendar: the Corkscrew
at Laguna Seca, California, where Marc famously
overtook Valentino Rossi (Yamaha).

Another historic moment in Marc's championship-
winning season. Thursday in Qatar – the first
day of official MotoGP training. Marc tries out
his Honda for real. Fourth in the first session;
first in the next two; second in the fourth; sixth
on the grid; third in the race itself, after battling
for second place with none other than Valentino
Rossi at the finishing line, both riders finishing
behind Jorge Lorenzo (Yamaha). And all at night.

Marc at the French Grand Prix, held at Le
Mans, home of the legendary 24-hour race for
sportscars.

Marc at the iconic Indianapolis circuit, where he won ahead of Dani Pedrosa (Honda) and Jorge Lorenzo (Yamaha).

The World Championship showcased the colourful new track at Austin, Texas, and Marc responded with overall victory and a new record as the youngest rider in history to win a GP in the senior class.

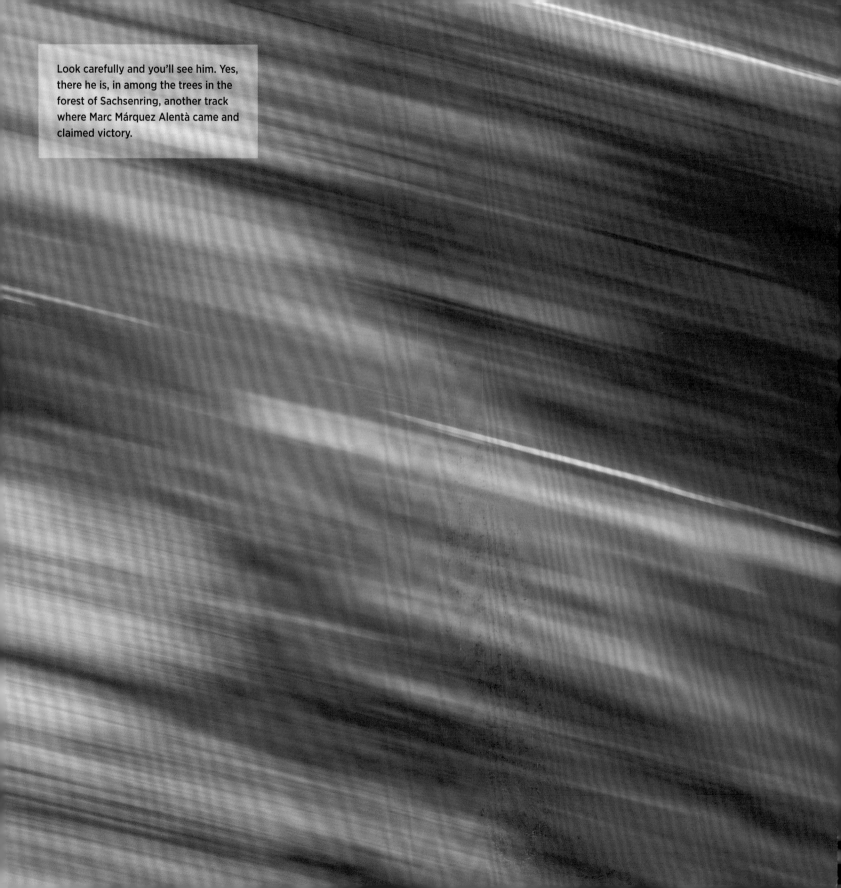

Look carefully and you'll see him. Yes, there he is, in among the trees in the forest of Sachsenring, another track where Marc Márquez Alentà came and claimed victory.

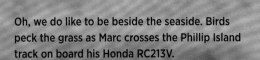
Oh, we do like to be beside the seaside. Birds peck the grass as Marc crosses the Phillip Island track on board his Honda RC213V.

Marc riding at almost 200mph, as seen through the trees at Laguna Seca on the left, and at Indianapolis on the right.

Pain and courage

Below, Marc injures himself in a fall (one of several) at Mugello, Italy, one of only two races where he came away with no points. Bottom, toppling over in the first practice at Phillip Island, Australia. In the main image, he rides to victory at Laguna Seca, California.

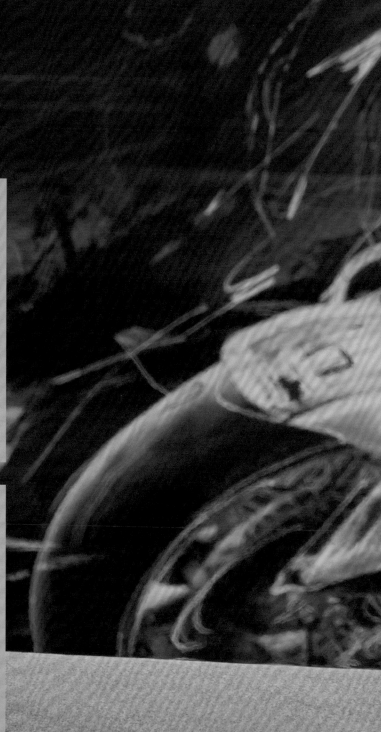

Surfing fans' heads

Wherever he goes, wherever he races, wherever he puts on a show, Marc has thousands of fans. Some say he's inheriting Valentino Rossi's followers, though that's never been his intention. In this photo, we see Marc in a training session at Australia, seeming to surf his powerful Honda over the heads of his supporters.

The modern tower at the new US circuit in Austin
provides a great vantage point for watching Marc
and Dani escape. On the right, the highly original
wall at Motorland, Aragón, provides the backdrop to
a duel between Jorge Lorenzo (Yamaha) and Marc,
which can also be seen on the next page.

There are many ways to win

Winning doesn't always mean coming first. Winning, according to Italy's Livio Suppo, one of the team managers at Repsol Honda, 'also means putting on a show'. Marc did not always win in 2013 (in 18 grand prixs, he had 16 podiums, 6 of them as winner), but he always gives the best of himself and his bike, and tries to please the public.

Above, Qatar, his MotoGP debut, where Marc finished third, losing out to Valentino Rossi in the final few yards. But Marc was also a winner in a way, just as he was a winner at Motegi, Japan, even though he finished second. These races can be seen on the next pages, followed by Marc at Aragón's Motorland, celebrating with a flag bearing the famous number 93 in front of fans and officials.

Laps of honour. On the left, Marc crowdsurfing with his team in the paddock at Sachsenring, Germany; on the right, diving into the arms of his team after winning at Brno, Czech Republic.

Santi Hernández, Marc's head coach, left, and
Julià, Marc's father, right, in a huddle to celebrate
Marc's victory at the Czech Republic Grand Prix.

Three people who were fundamental to Marc's 2013 MotoGP World Championship triumph. On the left, a kiss from Santi Hernández, Marc's head coach; Carlos Liñán, previously Marc's most trusted mechanic and now Marc's head mechanic, watches on, smiling with joy. On the right, Emilio Alzamora, the manager of the triple champion, accompanying his young charge through the corridors of the Indianapolis circuit.

Next pages: Marc's celebrations are very happy occasions. From the left: Qatar, Laguna Seca, Sachsenring, Aragón, Brno and Austin. On the right, one of the happiest moments of Marc's life, on the podium at Austin (after a record-breaking victory), spraying Santi Hernández, his head coach, with cava.

MotorLand Aragón 2013

Circuit of the Americas 20

Crying tears of joy, dripping with sweat

This image, so precise, exact and unique – another brilliant black-and-white photograph – is from the Malaysian Grand Prix, but it could be from any circuit, from any other race. But not from any other rider: for Marc Márquez Alenta that tear drop represents the pure pleasure of racing and entertaining others.

That drop, alongside the Repsol lettering, could also be a splash of petrol. Or the sweat of exertion, after chasing Dani Pedrosa (Honda), the eventual winner, and battling to finish second, in order to increase the margin between himself and Jorge Lorenzo (Yamaha), who came third.

Or it could be a drop of pleasure, knowledge and intuition, an understanding that he was getting close to achieving his ultimate goal. That drop sums this whole book up. A drop dangling from the chin of the most brilliant motorcyclist Spain has ever produced. From the chin of the champion of champions. From the best rookie in history.

The Red Sea

What follows is an extended party, the scenes of
celebration and ecstasy that followed events at Valencia's
Cheste circuit. Thus was Marc Márquez Alentà crowned
'king of kings', the best debut rider in history, the record-
breaker, the 200mph boy wonder.

What these pages show is the Red Sea of number
93; the speed king celebrating winning the World
Championship with his people, the happiest people in all
the world; making the sign of Number 1, surrounded by
photographers and then chased by race officials.

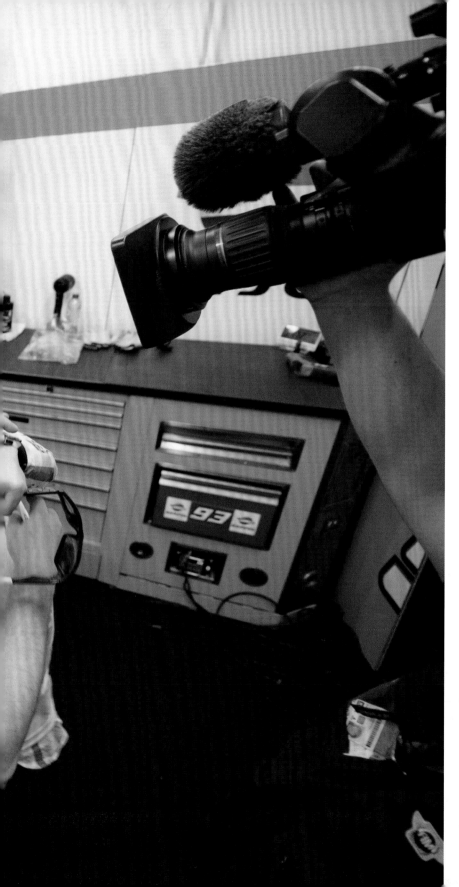

One big joyous party in the Repsol Honda pit enclosure at Cheste.
Family, team, friends and fans throw Marc in the air after winning
the MotoGP title.

The three gods of speed

Here we are. Take our picture. It's the home straight, the finishing line at Valencia, the moment of glory. The ultimate podium features Maverick Viñales as the winner of Moto3, Marc Márquez as the new king of MotoGP, and Pol Espargaró as champion of Moto2.

The image below was taken one hour later. Marc enters his trailer, accompanied by Anna Pagés, his press officer, to celebrate the title he's just won with his team. From his expression, and the way he's running his hand through his hair, he seems to be saying to himself, 'What have I done now?'

The rain, the thunderclaps and the flashes of lighting over Cervera can't spoil the party. The streets are packed, there's singing and celebration. 'And there'll be more to come, and there'll be more to come,' Marc shouted, raising his hands with his brother Àlex. And the champ was given the bumps, of course. And there were fireworks. And colour. Red. And Champions League-style ticker-tape. Because something like this, such an amazing achievement, could be celebrated no other way.

The awards ceremony where Marc Márquez was proclaimed MotoGP world champion and became the youngest rider ever to lift the premier category trophy. In the image on the left, Márquez is seen alongside Carmelo Ezpeleta, CEO of Dorna, the company that organises the World Championship; Venezuela's Vito Ippolito, President of the Federation of International Motorcycling (FIM); and Jorge Lorenzo and Dani Pedrosa, who completed the 2013 MotoGP podium. On the right, watched by Carmelo Ezpeleta in the background, Marc Márquez is presented with the trophy.

Authors

Mirco Lazzari
Castel San Pietro, Bologna, Italy, 1961

It's not easy being Mirco Lazzari. It's not easy on the heart, the mind, the sense of intuition and smell and everything else that makes him unique at the moment he hits the trigger on his Nikon to capture another distinctive, original and artistic image.

Every year since 2002, Lazzari has published a book called *Living at 200*, a sumptuous collection of photographs of the World Championship. This is his way of sharing with everyone what he carries in his heart, in his head and in his fingertips: the love of racing that his father Mario gave him, and the love of art, painting and photography that he got from his mother Francesca.

It was his mother who gave him his first little camera, and it was his father who took him to Imola, near where Mirco grew up, to see his first race. But it was Mirco who turned himself into a photographer of international standing, a fixture at prestigious agencies such as Allsport/Grazia and, more recently, GettyImages.

His partner, Raffaela Gianola, has an art degree and specialises in photography books. She's the one who takes the raw material of the images he captures and turns them into liquid gold.

Emilio Pérez de Rozas
Barcelona, Spain, 1952

Grandson of a photographer, son of a photographer, nephew of a photographer, brother of a photographer, a part-time photographer himself … Emilio Pérez de Rozas studied Information Sciences, part of the first generation to study journalism at Barcelona University. Learning from the likes of his brother, Carlos, from Antonio Franco and the late, lively and enterprising Alex J. Botines, Emilio decided to take the plunge and devote himself to sports journalism. He now writes for *Diario de Barcelona, El País* and *El Periódico de Catalunya.*

Thanks to the help and support of Juan Porcar, and the late José Luis Aznar, Emilio began covering the World Championship in the year when Freddie Spencer was winning 250cc and 500cc grand prix races on the same morning. Ángel Nieto was beginning his last lap, and Sito Pons and Joan Garriga would get the crowd out of their seats, but such days of Spanish glory were followed by a long period of drought, with the World Championship totally dominated by Anglo-Saxons – North Americans, Englishmen, Italians and Australians – until the tarmac rewarded Emilio with what has been a brilliant decade for Spanish motorcycling.

This is his third book following the exploits of Marc Márquez. The first, *Una mirada al mágico 2010 (A Look Back at the Magical 2010),* tells the story of the young champion's victory in the 125cc Championship, and the second, *Las manos mágicas (The Magic Hands),* recounts Marc's victory in the Moto2 Championship of 2012.